AN ENLIGHTENED
Life

Aldwyn Altuney
Christine Innes
Kleo Merrick
Larissa Beattie
Lisa Ohtaras
Marika Gare

Rosie Shalhoub
Sharon Le Fort
Steph Gobraiel
Terri Tonkin
Tracey Horton

The Corporate Escapists

Copyright © 2023 by Christine Innes

All rights reserved. No part of this book may be reproduced in any form on or by an electronic or mechanical means, including information storage and retrieval systems, without permission in writing from the publisher, except by a reviewer who may quote brief passages in a review.

This book is designed to provide information and inspiration to our readers. It is sold with the understanding that the publisher is not engaged to render any professional advice. The content of each month is the sole expression and opinion of its author and not necessarily that of the publisher. No warranties or guarantees are expressed or implied by the publishers' choice to include any of the content in this book. Neither the publisher nor the author(s) shall be liable for any physical, psychological, emotional, financial, or commercial damages including, but not limited to, special, incidental, consequential or other damages.

First printed 2023 by The Corporate Escapists.

Printed on-demand in Australia, United States and the United Kingdom.

Table of Contents

Introduction — v

Christine Innes — 2
Seen but not heard

Aldwyn Altuney — 16
Enlivened to enlighten

Kleo Merrick — 32
Permission to awaken

Larissa Beattie — 44
Embodying my purpose

Lisa Ohtaras — 58
An enlightened perspective of wounds

Marika Gare — 72
Journey to enlightenment

Rosie Shalhoub — 86
Embracing magick

Sharon Le Fort — 98
Standing strong

Steph Gobraiel — 112
The power of family: Re-defining success

Terri Tonkin — 126
Living on purpose

Tracey Horton — 138
Your purpose is always in a season

Introduction

Are you tired of feeling stuck in your life? Do you crave a deeper sense of purpose and fulfillment? Look no further than "An Enlightened Life," the inspiring new book by 11 incredible women from around the world.

Over the past few years, these authors have transformed their own lives with the help of coaches and mentors who acted as lighthouses, guiding them towards healing, growth, and success. Now, they want to pay it forward and act as lighthouses for you.

In this book, you'll discover the secrets to living an Enlightened Life. Through the personal stories and wisdom shared by these authors, you'll learn how to cultivate insight, openness, and clarity in your life by practicing daily habits that open your heart, mind, body, and soul.

Each chapter is filled with powerful insights and practical advice that will empower and inspire you to become the best version of yourself. From finding inner peace to showing gratitude and staying in the flow of life, these authors have got you covered.

If you're seeking a lighthouse to guide you through life's challenges, "An Enlightened Life" is the book for you. Don't miss out on the opportunity to transform your life and create the life and business of your dreams. Buy your copy today!

Love and light

x *Christine*

CHAPTER 1

Christine Innes

Seen but not heard

"DREAMS + ACTION = REALITY"
~ Christine Innes

To all the dreamers out there who need hope, inspiration and guidance.

Growing up it was said a lot, that kids were to be seen but not heard. We were to sit in the corner and play nicely and if we were to get a little rowdy, we were told to be quiet and keep our voices down.

As I grew up, I became quite vocal and was labeled as fog horn. The one who was the 'big kid' due to my size and also as I had the loudest voice.

Being told to "keep quiet", not seen, to "stand up and suck your gut in", and also to stand behind the others so no one can see how big you are.

It did have some damage on the inside. This year, as I turned 46, I realised that the words were literally that.. WORDS.

It was the emotions I felt for all of this time that made me become who I am today!

Talk about a 360

When I look back on who I was as a kid, teenager, young adult, and even who I was 1 year ago, I have changed completely - talk about a complete 360 change.

Even down to my hair colour, I have changed. Stepping into the real version of who I am has given me a sense of calm, sense of purpose and also shown me the light that was inside of me that needed to shine more.

I am a storyteller, a person who can take someone's story and give it light. I also use my own story to shine the light for others - to show them what is possible, to give them the strength, guidance, empowerment, and inspiration they need to own their story.

The 360 I have done in my life has not been easy, yet it has given me my power back.

I have been blessed over the past 4 years to work with some of the most incredible mentors. One of these mentors talks about how we all have the ability to pick up a pen and write our own stories, yet so many of us give that pen to someone else to write - we literally give the power of our own life away.

AN ENLIGHTENED *Life*

When I first heard that I sunk down low. It was the feeling of guilt and shame rising up as for at that time it was 38 years of my life I had been allowing others to write my own story.

Now, I have the pen in my hand and I am writing my own story.

Designing my own life

So how can someone take that pen and start to write their story? The key I learned is that you have to own your story. I mean the good, the not-so-good and the shit in between.

No one else needs to own it, except you. Now you don't need to stand in front of hundreds of people like I do or share in front of millions with your own YouTube channel, podcast or magazine like i do. What you do need to do is to be able to stand in front of the mirror and own it.

The mirror is your own reflection - the only one staring back is YOU. You are the judge, the inspiration, the owner, and the keeper of your story.

Taking ownership of of my story, was the first step to designing a life I love.

I needed to own...

The failed marriages
The illnesses changing how I live life
The bankruptcy
Sleeping on my parents' couch
Losing the life I thought I wanted
The loss of the (my? Instead of 'the') corporate identity as I did not know who I was

I needed to own it all before I could determine what I wanted and who I was.

When I did this I took that pen back and started to design a life on my own terms.

That life, which filled me with love, joy, abundance, happiness, and hope. A life that I created and did not let others dictate what I should be doing. A life that lit me up and allowed me to follow my dreams and passion.

Changing course - to happiness

At mum's surprise birthday, a relative asked me what I was doing with my life. It was the first time I could not answer the question. Strange for a person who never has a problem with talking - after all I was the fog horn of the family.

Afterwards I reflected on the question I was asked. In that moment, I remember a colleague talking about how she learned about a practice called 'An Ideal Day'. I had written about this practice many times with my clients, yet it had only just clicked that it was the key starting point for me to change course and choose a path to happiness.

An ideal day is about creating and visualising a day you cannot wait to wake up to, a day that sets your soul on fire.

Creating this day was the first step and from that day on I have continued to incorporate this practice in my annual routine. I absolutely love doing this.

What I have realised is that as I grow, learn more about myself, and sink into my own happiness, my ideal day changes.

AN ENLIGHTENED *Life*

It changes with who I want to spend my time with. It changes with the conversations I want to have, it changes with the clients I want to work with.

Because I am in charge of my life. I get to choose my own ideal day and I choose happiness.

The key part is that I choose to use my voice to share my story and not be quiet. I am not just being loud for the sake of it. I have a message that I want to share. I have something to say and it is important to ME to say it no matter how loud others think I am!

Happiness is around the corner

Owning my story was the first step to happiness, yet I always wonder how I could embrace it even more?

A few years ago I discovered the power of gratitude. Now, most people think with gratitude it is all about the good things you are grateful for. And yes, this is true, to fully step into happiness, I truly believe that you need to also be grateful for all the other stuff in your life - you know the things we need to own but tend to avoid or dismiss.

I wouldn't be the person I am today without being grateful for the good, the not so good things and all the stuff in between that has happened in my life.

In the earlier part of the chapter I mention this as part of owning your story, yet to reach true happiness we also need to be grateful for it.

Accept it, be grateful for what it is teaching you as it is all part of the process of how we ultimately become the person we want to be accepted as - our true selves.

We all want acceptance, yet acceptance has to start with self - warts and all!

Forgiveness and forgiveness of self

After the gratitude, comes forgiveness. Most of us, say the word "sorry', and it can have little to no meaning at all. Forgiveness goes deep and can reach your soul.

Learning forgiveness of one's self and others, gives us the next layer of happiness.

It took me a long time to understand that I need forgiveness to move forward. The forgiveness allowed me to see the 'moment' for what it was.

I use the word 'moment' as the only thing that lasts forever is death. So everything we go through is a 'moment' in life and does not last forever.

Learning the practice of forgiveness to reach deep into my soul has also learnt (taught) me to heal, grow, and be the best version of myself.

It is the lessons from all of the moments. My spiritual teacher taught me early on in my personal growth journey: "It is happening for you, not to you".

I can hear you saying now - 'it is so hard to understand and also accept this' when you are right in the middle of a shit storm.

It is one of the best things that you can do!

I mean, in 2015, I was diagnosed with 2 life changing illnesses, left a toxic and unfixable marriage, filed for bankruptcy, and ended up sleeping on my parents' couch.

AN ENLIGHTENED *Life*

IT SUCKED and IT WAS happening TO ME.

Yet now as I reflect back, it was the best thing that happened and I can see that it did happen 'for me' for many reasons

For me to grow
For me to appreciate my own life
For me to appreciate what I have
For me to appreciate what I can do and have for myself.

That moment in life was a blessing in disguise that helped me take the first steps to changing the course of my life.

Now I practice the art of forgiveness at a soul level so I can let go, heal myself, and see the lessons in each moment.

A new way of life

Learning the art of gratitude and forgiveness has shown me how to fully step into my own power, use my voice and realise that all I have been through is a gift. It has shown me that I can help so many others do the same.

I have a voice and I have a story to tell. I am going to tell it to whom I want , not sit quietly in the corner.

My new way of life is living it to the fullest. I got a big reality check as I truly thought I had been doing this.

Then last year in September my dad passed away. I could have frozen and completely stopped living life, however, instead I stepped deep into my practice of gratitude and forgiveness, and it got me through one of the toughest and emotional times of my life.

Sadly nothing can bring my dad back and unfortunately, he won't be able to do all the things life has in store for us. What I do know though is that I am still here and can do all the things and my gratitude and forgiveness practices have given me the gift to be able to see that and make the decision to play full out.

My Dad was a beacon for me so the best way I can honour his life is to play full out and shine brightly.

When I talk about this to family and friends I get a gentle nod.

This is why I am sharing this.

Death, brings up your own mortality.
Death, shows you how fragile life is.
Death, shows you how short life is.

My dad is no longer here to have the beautiful conversations with people he loves, he can no longer see or play with his grandchildren and great grandson, follow his dreams, take the holidays he desires or be with his loved ones.

I CAN

I am no longer wasting a minute.

Are you?

Playing Full Out

Not a concept most people would think about, yet hearing my story, I hope it gives you a glimpse into your own life to play full out. To follow your dreams and live YOUR life.

AN ENLIGHTENED *Life*

Playing full out also comes with the realisation that maybe we have more healing to do, we have new dreams, new desires, new hobbies, new friendships, new love to explore.

Whatever it is for you, the key pathway is to create a day you love, give gratitude, allow in forgiveness and play full out in every aspect of your life.

During the time my dad was sick before he passed, I had a moment where I could choose to play full out and I took it

I invested in my business growth and backed myself.

It has paid off and each day I wake up and ask the universe to show me how good it can get as I am ready to play full out.

Each day is a blessing, and your mindset, your own personal growth will give you the tools you need to own your story and play full out.

Just one simple question - are you ready to do it?

5 steps to owning your story

1. Gratitude is your new attitude.

    I love the book 'The Secret' as it touches on gratitude and how to write a gratitude journal each day. What I have taken away from this book is that we also need to be grateful for what we have and what we have experienced.

    Each day write down 10 things you are grateful for.

    It could be;

    I am truly grateful for my health, because I get to wake up each day and live it with passion and play full out.

I am truly grateful for going through bankruptcy, because it gave me a new start on life and also allowed me to appreciate all I have now and how I can show my clients the power of owning their story.

2. Forgiveness of Self and others to allow the goodness in.

    Let's start with Self. During the day, watch how you speak to yourself, how you might criticise yourself and forgive yourself for this.

    I remember when I hit my toe, I said, "you stupid idiot Christine". Not pleasant yet it was my inner talk coming out.

    When I catch myself saying things like this, I use part of the famous Ho'oponopono prayer

    I am sorry, please forgive me, thank you, l love you.

    Ask yourself, would you speak to your best friend like that? - if no, then why talk to yourself like that?

3. Dream big.

    Don't forget to dream big. Most of us have been sitting in the back corner, keeping quiet. Quiet of our own dreams, our goals, the life we want.

    Take 10 minutes to 1 hour, or as long as you need to think of the dreams you would like to achieve in your life.

    DREAM BIG

4. Take action.

    Now from those dreams, what are 1 or 2 you could do right now? Could you book that holiday, could you apply for the new job, could you start the business?

AN ENLIGHTENED *Life*

When we take action the universe listens and so does our brain and it helps us bring in the opportunities, the people, the connections we need to achieve our dreams. The action starts with YOU!

5. Watch it become reality.

Are you like me and a bit impatient? I sit at a 10/10 when it comes to being impatient, mainly because I appreciate time and especially my life.

Learning the art of watching and waiting is key to allowing us to appreciate the moments. All the moments in life, the good and no so good, as this is what makes us who we are.

When you get a bit impatient, take a step back and remind yourself that some things take time. While you are doing that, say a few affirmations to remind yourself of the person you are.

Here are a few examples of affirmations I use:

YOU ARE AMAZING
YOU ARE LOVED
YOU ARE WORTHY
YOU ARE YOU

Keep shining

DREAMS + ACTION = REALITY

Love and light

x Christine

Christine Innes

The Corporate Escapists

Christine Innes is a Coach, Speaker, #1 International Best Seller Author, host of The Corporate Escapists Podcast, and editor-in-chief of The Corporate Escapists Magazine.

Christine is the CEO and Founder of The Corporate Escapists, a global company empowering people to transform their lives by letting go of their corporate identity and finding and following their passion.

Christine's clients say:

"I have been lucky to be featured in the magazine, however, what I cherished the most is that Christine has held my hand through the process of rebranding. I love it! I highly recommend anyone wishing to have a fabulous take in a new direction to call Christine, she is a champion through and through." - Dr. Anne-Marie

"Christine has been our business coach at Curious Me for several months. Wow, what a difference one-on-one coaching makes! Christine gave us the inspiration, motivation, and accountability we needed to go from planning for the now, to see the future. We started setting ourselves serious business goals and with her help, put in place action plans and timelines to make it happen. We experienced our best financial quarter EVER, even with COVID interruptions. all thanks to her help. We are forever grateful for Christine, her support, mentorship, and friendship." - Curious Me

Christine is passionate about helping people be themselves and create a life they love.

Christine offers 1:1 coaching with her two signature programs:

EmpowHER: A 12-week program helping you go from corporate mess to your empowHERed best

The Corporate Kickoff Program: A 60-day program to launch your business online.

Facebook: @christineinnescoach @thecorporateescapists
Instagram: @christine_innes @thecorporateescapists
Website: www.thecorporateescapists.com

CHAPTER 2

Enlivened to enlighten

Impacted by negative news

Born in 1974, I grew up in a loving household of Greek, Turkish and Ukrainian heritage. As all three countries have been at war with each other over the previous century, I jokingly call myself the 'love child' now!

Growing up in Sydney's northern beaches watching at least two hours of mainly negative mainstream news each night at home, I grew up angry and depressed with the state of the world. I felt invisible and that I didn't belong here for many years. I also felt hopeless and helpless to do anything about it.

I remember one night after watching the news in our house in North Balgowlah, I was so disturbed by it, I cried my eyes out and went up to my dad and asked: "Why are people so cruel? Why is the world like this?"

He hugged me and said: "Darling, that's just how the world is."

For a long time, I believed him.

I soon found plenty of evidence in my life of the cruelty I saw daily in the news. My innocence was lost at the age of six on my first and last family trip to Turkey. I befriended a beautiful big sheep at my grandma's house, which I later witnessed being killed in front of me.

What I wasn't told and I wouldn't have understood as a six-year-old is that what happened was a Greek orthodox tradition that when family come from a long way away, they sacrifice a sheep as an offering to God and to feed the poor people in the village.

When I returned to North Balgowlah Public School that year, I was bullied by fellow students. They picked on me because of my name, the food I took to school and the clothes I wore. Anything they could pick on, they did.

Internalising my anger led to depression

My dad said to me at a young age that 'anger is danger' and I internalised my anger for years, which led to depression.

When he introduced me to table tennis, I found an outlet to release my anger through the sport and developed a killer forehand smash.

AN ENLIGHTENED *Life*

Soon, I became the number one ranked Australian junior table tennis player and toured Australia and internationally for six years.

Not feeling like I belonged anywhere, I also started rebelling from a young age and began running away from home at age 13.

At age 15, my dad was fed up with my constant rebellion. When I arrived home around 5am the morning after a Halloween party, he kicked me out of the house.

The grass is not always greener on the other side

I moved into a crazy household in Manly that day, with a drug-addicted drummer, his alcoholic mother and drug-dealing sister.

It was a complete party house with non-stop music and jamming until sunrise each morning. After six months of this, with my boyfriend lying and cheating, the final straw was seeing my best friend kissing and cuddling him on our bed. I called my mum in tears and she graciously invited me to 'come home'. My dad gave me another chance and I ended up studying very hard alongside my brother Nicholas.

I had gone from Dux of North Balgowlah Primary School to failing everything in Year 11 at Mosman High School. I changed schools at the start of Year 12 to Forest High School, which was another turning point in my life. I began appreciating my parents and family much more.

I ended up qualifying to do a Bachelor of Arts in Communication (Media) degree at the University of Canberra (UC) from 1992 to 1994.

True love or was it?

In Canberra, I met my first true love - a man I thought I would be together with for life. He was four years older than me, a creative artist and sculptor. We got along famously and soon moved in together.

While at uni, the role of Editor of the university newspaper, CUrio, became available. I applied three times before I was offered the position. I took the fortnightly publication from 24 pages to 48 pages and had 30 contributors, which I co-ordinated.

I became the longest serving editor at the paper and loved the power the media had to affect change in the community. I found the media was a great way to share my voice on what I felt were injustices in the world and ways to help make it a better place to live. I wrote a story about anti-duck shooting, with the headline 'Go and Get Ducked!' and about issues that moved me in some way, including battery farming of chickens, female circumcision and stories about protecting the environment.

I graduated with High Distinctions in TV Production and Photojournalism.

Being very ambitious and not liking the icy cold weather in Canberra, my boyfriend and I moved to Brisbane in 1995. I soon secured casual and part-time jobs as a graphic designer, reporter for Rave, Time Off and Artika publications, market researcher, photographer and telemarketer.

Notice the warning signs

Growing up believing I had to work hard for my money, I was working crazy hours and my boyfriend of four years kept politely asking me to spend more time with him. Repeatedly, I ignored him until one night, when I arrived home around 5am after a photography gig, he jumped out of bed half asleep.

A tall, strong man, he pushed me against the wall in a psycho hypnotic state, strangled me and almost killed me. When I eventually broke free of his hold on my neck, shocked and in terror again, I bawled my eyes out. I was 22. He soon apologised but it was too late. I had already lost trust in him and the relationship.

Within one month, I was offered a full-time job as a Journalist at the Daily Mercury in Mackay. I left my boyfriend and pursued my career.

This was the start of what ended up being a lucrative career in the media for me. I went on to work as a journalist on TV, in radio and print media across Australia and internationally. Since then, I have interviewed stars including Charlie Sheen, Jewel, Vanilla Ice, Hugh Jackman, Russell Crowe, Cyndi Lauper, Debbie Harry (Blondie), Alby Mangels and Jimmy Barnes, among others.

After two years at The Daily Mercury, I worked at the Coffs Harbour Advocate, Queensland Times in Ipswich, Satellite Newspapers in Brisbane, Rave and Time Off in Brisbane, the Gold Coast Bulletin and Sun Community Newspapers (as a Journalist/Sub Editor for five years).

I did work experience at Channel 7 and ABC TV in Brisbane and hosted radio shows at 4CRM in Mackay, 2CHY in Coffs Harbour and Life FM on the Gold Coast (now Juice 1073).

As fate would have it

When I first moved to the Gold Coast in January 2000, I never planned to stay there. My goal was always to live in America, so I rented apartments for the first two years.

I found a beautiful beachfront unit in Main Beach and gave a guy about $1000 in rent and bond money - believing him to be the owner.

It turns out, he was renting and owed three weeks in rent!"

I could not believe someone would do that or that I fell for such a con artist!

I decided to not rent anymore and bought a house in Southport on the Gold Coast, which I still live in - 21 years on. This turned out to be a blessing in disguise.

I believe in karma. What comes around, goes around 10-fold - and not necessarily by the same people who rip others off or do harm! If you want great things to happen in your life, do great things for others.

Passionate about inspiring truth & good news

I started my business AA Xposé Photography in 2002 on the Gold Coast after having a few small car accidents working late nights with a photography company in Brisbane.

During the day, I was a journalist at the Sun Newspapers. When I left that position in 2005, the business evolved into AA Xposé Media as people began requesting public relations work, copywriting, video, graphic design, editing and media training services.

I did my first media training workshops in 2003 and had repeated calls for more.

In 2005, I invested $7000 in my first personal development course in the Hunter Valley, NSW. To this day, 18 years later, I have invested more than $500,000 in business and marketing courses, as well as many different modalities of personal development. This has been invaluable for the growth of my business and myself and has given me great insight into the decisions I have made in life and the meaning I have given to it.

Mass Media Mastery program launches globally

In 2014, I launched an online media training program called Mass Media Mastery, where I teach people how to get free publicity and mass media exposure.

Members of my Mass Media Mastery program are from all over Australia and overseas; including the Netherlands, South Africa, the US, UK and NZ. They are small business owners, authors, speakers, coaches and social entrepreneurs.

I help people who have a great message, product or service to share it with the masses using online and offline media so they can build their credibility in the community, business, sales and leave a legacy. In 2021, I also launched Free Publicity Secrets and Social Media Masterclasses.

As I have had depression over the years and four friends take their own lives by the age of 45, I am also passionate about promoting more good news stories in the mass media to help decrease depression and suicide rates worldwide, and lift people's spirits. In line with this, I founded a worldwide Good News Day on August 8, 2018, and the monthly Global Good News Challenge in June 2020.

The day that changed my life

It was a beautiful sunny day on February 19, 2023, and I was excited to be going for a four wheel drive on the beach for the first time.

I was invited by my good friend, Angelique Pellegrino, from Brisbane, who I met after she joined my Mass Media Mastery program in 2021.

We co-hosted a workshop together the day before called Open Your Mind to Flourish in Coffs Harbour at a spectacular multi-million dollar home, which the attendees loved.

Angelique's son, Daniel Pellegrino, and his girlfriend, Charlotte King, were also in town, staying with us at the spectacular Pacific Bay Resort and they invited me to join them on this 4WD beach trip.

At 12.30pm, we began driving along Boambee Beach at a steady pace with the windows open and a beautiful strong breeze coming over us. The sky was clear blue and the ocean looked absolutely spectacular.

We were laughing, having a great time, taking photos and enjoying some drinks.

We toasted to life and expressed gratitude for all its blessings.

AN ENLIGHTENED *Life*

Boambee Beach is 5.7km long from Boambee headland and creek in the south to Gallows Beach and Corambirra point in the north.

When we arrived at the end of the beach to the creek, we noticed about five other 4wd vehicles parked nearby. There were no swimmers, surfers or boats in the ocean and no lifeguards.

The water was shallow in this beautiful creek that flowed into the ocean about 100 metres to the left, coming up to knee height.

Angelique, Daniel and Charlotte floated down the creek first. As the trio walked back up towards me, I hopped into the creek and off I went.

Laying on my back, I flowed smoothly down the left side of the creek past them and soon stopped at the end where the sand had banked up.

Thinking 'oh that was fun', I stood up and walked a few steps into the middle of the creek to float down a bit further.

With my eyes partially closed to block out the sun, the next thing I knew, a massive wave came crashing down over my head and the sand fell away beneath me.

The wave swept me out to sea, followed by another massive wave that came over me, then another one and another one.

I was being taken out further and further to sea by these waves and a strong undercurrent, further away from the rock wall - my nearest sign of safety.

I couldn't touch the sand under the water and began to panic. As the waves kept coming over me, some of them I swam under and some, I floated above.

I was shocked and thought it must be a rip, so I'll just go with it.

"Don't fight it," I was telling myself, believing that eventually I would come back around the waves like I'd done with so many other rips that I had been in before.

However this wasn't like any other rip I'd been caught in before, because the waves continued going over my head and the sweeping undertow kept taking me further and further out to sea away from the headland.

I thought, 'surely these waves will eventually stop, the current will stop pulling me out and eventually, I'll be able to swim across the waves and come on to the rocks', but they didn't.

Before I knew it, I was about a kilometre out from the shore and a long way from the headland.

I couldn't see beneath the ocean as it was very dark under the waves and choppy seas and I was paranoid about sharks.

At this point, I was so far out that when I looked back to the shore, the four wheel drives were tiny.

I noticed Daniel's black jeep going very fast along the beach from the creek back towards the beach entrance.

I felt some relief believing he was seeking help but was still petrified that at any moment, I could be taken by a shark.

Looking around frantically for anyone in or on the ocean, I was all alone.

I couldn't see any way I could get back to shore without exhausting myself. Knowing that if I tried to swim out of the waves, I would run out of breath and potentially die in the middle of the ocean.

So many conversations were going through my head, such as 'Have I manifested this because I said the ocean would be a good way to die to friends in the past?', 'Why did I say yes to Angelique to come to Coffs Harbour?' 'Is this going to be my last day on the planet?'

I had just turned 49 and I was not ready to die yet.

Tears started flowing down my cheeks, I looked up to the sky and prayed for help, then let go again and reconciled myself with thoughts such as 'How is this happening for you?' and 'What are the learnings in this?'

Then doing my best to breathe deeply and relax my body while looking down at the waves and my surroundings, keeping an eye out for sharks.

After more than an hour treading water and navigating the waves, I saw a surfer coming towards me from the rocks on a longboard. A guy called Shane, an ex lifesaver who was having a relaxing Sunday with family.

He helped me climb on to his board and within minutes, two jet ski riders arrived - the father son pair of Rod and Flynn Saville, who hadn't been at that beach for more than a year!

I climbed on to the jet ski with Shane's help and rode with Rod back to shore safely.

Angelique hugged me as I landed and I bawled my eyes out in tears. I said: "I'm so grateful to be here and to be alive."

As I placed my feet on the sand, I felt stable and safe again.

I reflected on this terrifying experience in the middle of nowhere panicking about sharks, which Boambee Beach is known for.

Four people drowned in New South Wales oceans that weekend, bringing the state's 2022-23 summer drowning death toll to a record number of 26 people all up.

I could easily have been number 27.

The learnings

1. Let go and let flow - adapt to your environment
2. Have faith and fun with life's curveballs. Fighting it is futile
3. Relax and trust yourself and others. Know that everything is in divine order
4. Keep good company. Teamwork makes the dream work
5. Swim between the flags, particularly if you swim in the ocean on your own
6. Research an area before you swim in the ocean
7. Learn how to calm your fears with practices like meditation, yoga and breathwork
8. Invest in yourself - the personal development work I've done has been invaluable to enabling me to survive this situation
9. Appreciate the miracle you are and be grateful for every moment
10. Realise that everything you do has a ripple effect on those around you
11. Live life to the fullest, even if it means taking some chances and finding yourself in deep water sometimes. Overcoming

challenges makes us stronger and remember, diamonds are created under pressure.

We are never alone - our ancestors are with us

I feel a strong drive and support for what I do from my ancestors. Scientifically, it is proven that we carry the DNA of 14 generations. My great grandparents were two of the 30,000 Kulaks executed by Stalin's men in the Ukraine in the early 1930s. As part of the mass eradication of Kulaks as a class, they were hanged outside their house on their farm in Kiev.

My grandfather was in another part of the Ukraine at the time and started to speak up about it until his friends said: "Because you're speaking up against the government, they are coming to kill you now." He then ran away to Turkey and met my dad's mum, who was Greek.

I know my ancestors are supporting me spiritually in helping others to stand up in life and speak their truth.

"Be the change you want to see in the world," as Gandhi said.

And I say: "Shine bright and light up all those around you."

Here's to your success! May you always make the most of every moment in this precious life and live 'an enlightened life' that you and your loved ones will be proud of.

Love and live fully,

Aldwyn

xox

Aldwyn Altuney

AA Xposé Media

Aldwyn Altuney is a mass media marketing expert.

Known as the Media Queen, she is a TV host, speaker, photojournalist and author of multiple international best-selling books.

With 39 years of media experience, her PR company, AA Xposé Media, is the only one she knows of that guarantees results in the mainstream media.

She is passionate about inspiring more good news in the mass media to help decrease depression and suicide rates and lift people's spirits.

In 2018, she founded the Mass Media Tribe and Gold Coast Business Laughter Club Meetup groups.

She also founded the global Good News Day in 2018, which is run annually on August 8, and the monthly Global Good News Challenge in June 2020.

Also an animal activist, she founded Animal Action Events in 2007 and has run 16 annual charity events so far raising awareness, appreciation and respect for all animals.

In her spare time, she loves performing in her comedy duo The Fiddly Gigglers, acting, playing ukulele, long beach walks and body surfing.

As a stand for truth, good news and animal welfare, one of her favourite sayings is by Gandhi: "Be the change you wish to see in the world."

Connect: www.linktr.ee/aldwyn

CHAPTER 3

Kleo Merrick

Permission to awaken

"Live your best life for you, unapologetically"
~ Kleo Merrick

To Olga, you are my inspiration to keep moving forward.

My life has not been my own for 43 years.

No, I haven't been a slave or refugee where privileges had been stripped from me, nor do I wish to compare myself to any of the horrors that they go through.

Mine was a different type of violation, one in which I gave all my power away without even noticing.

Kleo Merrick

In coaching or spiritual terms, I was known as a 'rescuer'. The kind of person that would always go out of their way to help everyone else, even someone they didn't even know.

Some would argue, "that's a perfect way of being" and "more people should be like you!".

Unfortunately, what that meant was overly helping everyone else and never leaving anything for myself, or my family unit.

I was left empty.

There was no energy left for me, I was constantly drained and exhausted.

Not only that, but I was angry because I had done it again.

I let myself be overpowered by other people's needs, above my own.

And that had been the story of my life for 43 years.

But not anymore and never again…

For I have awakened…

And there's no putting a lid back on this beautiful, spiritual, and powerful being!

I grew up in an environment where I did as I was told, period.

There was no arguing, no conversation, no flexibility, no answering back and if you did, there was punishment.

My world was emotionally and mentally stifling.

AN ENLIGHTENED *Life*

Me and my siblings' thoughts, wants, needs and desires were completely ignored.

Neither my parents nor my grandparents had the time, patience, or awareness to raise children with the emotional intelligence that we have today.

The only time I was praised is when I did something good, for someone else.

But I wouldn't be praised directly, I would overhear the praise mentioned to other members of my family at parties and gatherings. Turned out that I was a 'good girl'.

Unfortunately, the same would occur with the 'bad stuff' that I'd done. There would be hushed whispers, suspicious looks, and gasping, in my direction.

Nope, I was wrong, turned out that I was a 'naughty little girl'.

What I noticed growing up was, that when I was a 'good girl' I was accepted as part of the family. They seemed to take ownership of my character and patted themselves on the back for having done such an amazing job raising me.

When, however, I was a 'naughty girl', that was solely my fault. And they took no responsibility as to why that may have occurred. Saying I must have got it from 'that Aunt' or another obscure relative that we never spoke to.

Growing up in my household was tough and I quickly learned that to survive in this environment I would always need to be the 'good girl'.

Failure to do so would mean unacceptance, neglect, not belonging, and not being loved.

So, I became a people pleaser to ensure that I was always a 'good girl'.

Just like everyone wanted.

Simple, right?

Wrong.

Running this behaviour and pattern of pleasing people and always being good, worked great for a while. Especially when I was little and desperately needed the approval of my family.

But when my teenage years hit, I unleashed my inner asshole!

13 years of pent-up emotion that had been neglected, overlooked, unsaid, controlled, ignored and all buried so deep into my inner soul had erupted like a raging volcano.

No one knew what hit them.

"What happened to our good girl" they would say. "She's changed, and did you hear what she did…?"

And life went back to overhearing hurtful remarks in hushed tones and judgmental looks at family outings.

The only difference now was, I didn't care what anyone thought of me.

The anger and rage were overpowering, and I just unleashed, yelling, slamming doors, retaliating, and fighting with everything I had.

At the time I had no idea what I was fighting against or whom, I had no conscious awareness of why I was even so angry.

AN ENLIGHTENED *Life*

Even though I'd always sort their approval, I certainly didn't need it now.

But that's just the problem, isn't it?

Because I did care.

I still cared so much, about what they thought, what I did, how I behaved towards them and the shocked looks on their faces.

And almost every night that I can remember, I cried myself to sleep, praying life would be bearable tomorrow.

But it wasn't.

For a long time, life just seemed to go from horrible to slightly bearable.

There was the occasional day when it was good, but that was because of my siblings and friends, and nothing to do with my peers.

I spent years feeling angry, hating myself for being angry and aggressive and then feeling guilty about feeling angry.

So, it would go around in a circle, round, and round with no end in sight.

I didn't know how to break the cycle, I had no help, so support, and no understanding.

Whilst I exploded, my siblings were trying to deal with their own problems in their own ways too, some were in denial, others shut down, and others created a fantasy world.

Each of us doing our best to escape the certainty of unreasonable judgments and harsh criticism from our peers.

Like a mouse frantically spinning its wheel in the cage, not knowing how to get out.

I had two personalities, the one my friends saw at school where I was happy. And the one at home when I was alone and miserable.

Something had to change.

In my mid-teens, I could have sleepovers at friends' houses. I loved the opportunity to escape my household and not be at home for a night. And for weeks I was on my best behaviour to ensure that I would be allowed to go.

By staying at other friends' homes, I started to notice that their families were nothing like mine.

The biggest difference was the parents would 'talk with' their children, as opposed to 'yell at' their children and they *actively listened* to their children.

They would ask for their opinions and have discussions at the dining table. Where the conversations would go both ways between the parents and the children.

They genuinely took an interest in each other's lives, thoughts, challenges, and aspirations.

I never knew families could be like this and didn't believe this at first.

After staying over at most of my girlfriends' houses, I noticed the same thing.

Each family had varying degrees of emotional intelligence and acceptance of their children, where they were seen as equals, but they still had it.

AN ENLIGHTENED *Life*

It was very much the opposite at my house, there was yelling, condescension, judgement, and berating and most of the meals were eaten in silence, fear, and quiet desperation.

It was there that I swore to myself that I would do better.

Knowing full well that I would totally fall flat on my face, most of the time, but I didn't care!

I would learn, challenge myself at every opportunity, and become a better version of myself.

And with that decision, the cycle was broken.

We can't run from our past, we must face it

As the years flew by from my late teens in the past, to now in my early 40's many things in my life have changed.

None of which were more significant than the arrival of my daughter.

We got off to a very rocky start as I was negotiating who I was as a parent.

Even though I fought so hard against it, I naturally fell into the unresourceful behaviours of my parents, as my only reference point.

I had ignored her, just as I had been.

I had dismissed her, just as I had been.

I had berated, expected, judged, and yelled.

I was a terrible mother and I hated myself for it.

And that's the thing about the past, you can't change it, you can't run from it. The only thing you can do, when you wish, is to learn from it.

We were driving in the car, and I listened to myself yelling at her like I was outside of my own body and inside that of my daughter.

I was the child again, hearing myself yelling with a child's voice and everything I was saying echoed from the past.

It was everything that I wanted to say to my mother when I was five and I couldn't.

I wouldn't dare.

It was everything that I tried to say as a teenager but couldn't find the language because it was so blurred with eruptions of suppressed emotions.

The car stopped; I had pulled over.

My voice was hoarse from shouting and my face was wet with tears.

My daughter at this point was just looking at me, wondering what was going to happen next.

I let go. I cried. I apologised.

We cried together. We hugged each other and we never looked back.

I stopped expecting her to be the 'good girl' all the time and realised kids, like adults, are complicated and individual and there's not only one right way of doing something.

AN ENLIGHTENED *Life*

Ultimately, we are both individual souls, that have each chosen to exist together in this lifetime.

All we all want is love, unconditionally.

Even though I could not have this in my past, I could certainly offer this to my daughter now for both of our futures.

For me, that's the best awakening I could ever have.

Currently five and a half years old, going on 25! She is my greatest teacher, transparent feedback giver, reflective mirror, and ultimate transformer.

Meeting her beautiful soul and bearing witness to her unfathomable ability to love has been the most wonderful challenge I've ever faced.

At the beginning of this chapter, I spoke about how I've been living my life for others.

Unknowingly allowing past influencers to control my actions and my future, while secretly still desperate for their approval.

For those of you that have found yourself in a similar situation, from my heart to yours… You do deserve a better life on your terms.

Kleo Merrick

I want to share with you my mantra:

I'm awake now, I see you.
I refuse to give you a footing in my past, my present or my future.
I will no longer please you or anyone.
I will strive to overcome my obstacles.
I will challenge myself to become a better version of myself.
I will live for myself.
I'm awake now, I see myself.
I am limitless.
I am powerful.
I have awakened.

Thank you all for reading,

Live your life for you,

Kleo xxx

Kleo Merrick

Merrick Courses Pty Ltd

Kleo Merrick is a 4-time Amazon #1 International Bestselling Author, Speaker, and Freelance Content & Marketing Strategist.

Kleo is the CEO of Merrick Courses, a company she founded in 2013 where she runs successful Workshops, Online Training Programs and teaches businesses how to market their services with Sales Funnels, Webinars and Online Courses. And educates them on how to manoeuvre Digital Marketing specifically for Entrepreneurs.

Her clients say: "Kleo taught me more in 2 hours than it would have taken me 5 years to learn myself…!!!" – Cathy Kingsley

She is the author of:

~ 'An Empowered Life: 10 Inspirational Stories From Women Around the World Who Have Dared to Live and Empowered Life',

~ 'An Inspired Life: 10 Inspirational Stories From Women Around the World Who Have Dared to Follow Their Passion',

~ 'I Did It: 16 Mindset Secrets To Transform The Life You Have Into The Ultimate Life you Desire',

~ 'Yes, I Can: 16 Success Secrets Form Inspiring Women Around The World', and

~ 'Compelling Selling: How To Earn More By Selling Less'.

Kleo is extremely passionate about Creating a Community of Passionate Business Owners and Upskilling them in the Digital World.

Email:	kleo@kleomerrick.com
Facebook:	www.facebook.com/marketingwithkleo/
Instagram:	www.instagram.com/kleomerrick/
LinkedIn:	www.linkedin.com/in/kleomerrick/
Website:	www.kleomerrick.com

CHAPTER 4

Larissa Beattie

Embodying my purpose

"To fully embody the light you must completely understand the dark" ~ *Larissa Beattie*

To my children, Ellyse and Damion, for always accepting my energetic highs and lows and bringing so much joy into my life.

And to my younger self, thank you for pushing through the hard times and the really tough times.

Inner knowing

I have had many awakenings in my lifetime, some small and some truly unmeasurable. Each of these experiences have been guided by a conversation I had with myself at the age of 15 years. I didn't know who I was talking with at the time but the voice came from outside my own head. The words were not my thoughts but very clearly within my mind. It all started on a day no different to any other. I was walking to school pondering my existence as any 15 year old does, when I asked myself 'What am I here for?' Instantly the question was answered.

'You are here for something big'.

Now these words might not sound like anything life changing or insightful but the energy, the vibration that filled and flowed through my body was almost crippling and it stopped me in my tracks. My body tingled and my legs went to jelly but still held me upright.

As a 15 year old I didn't know what this meant but I did know it was important by the way it made me feel and the underlying sense of serenity and deep knowing that everything would be ok. It's this deep inner knowing and those words that have driven much of my life, a trust or faith in the bigger picture that whatever direction my life went that it would all work out.

Underlying every big decision, conscious or unconscious, were the words 'You are here for something big'. So I said yes to the opportunities that came my way. Some opportunities I created through hard work, others just appeared. Amongst these opportunities were many obstacles and life challenges.

My first challenge was 22 years long and that was spent serving in the Royal Australian Air Force as an Avionics Technician. Many others came and went, all impacting, shaping and defining me. At the age of 21, my 23 year old boyfriend was killed in a motorbike accident. Life stood still for many months as I dealt with this grief on my own but also exploring the side of me that woke up when he passed. My ability to communicate with spirit and with him was turned on.

This was my first awakening. My second awakening occurred after the birth of my daughter whilst suffering severe postnatal depression. I realised in my darkest hour that the only person that could help me was myself. In this moment energy flooded my body and a sense of love and nurture surrounded me. I knew everything was going to be ok. My third and what I call my first mass awakening occurred some years later when I met my then spiritual teacher. Overnight multiple senses and abilities were turned on. I could feel and see energy, hear my guides, speak thousands of different light languages, conduct psychic surgery and intense healings and the knowings of universal knowledge was overwhelming.

There are many more mass awakenings and stories to tell and I will get to them soon.

My human existence

I never questioned my upbringing and to me it was normal. Two loving parents that are still together today, and two younger sisters. My dad served in the Air Force and my mum ran her own business looking after young children in our home.

I didn't mind the other kids in the home, it gave me the opportunity to be on my own as I would hide in my room. What I did mind was having to change schools and move interstate every 3 years when my dad received a posting. Starting a new school was never easy. The new kid was always the target of bullies and I experienced my fair share of their lack of self worth and anger.

It was these lessons in life that saw me build a large wall over my heart. Never truly letting friends in because I knew I would have to leave them behind at some stage. I kept myself on the outer of the groups and focused nearly all of my attention on playing whatever sport came my way but my main love was playing hockey. Hockey was my escape to an alternate reality, one that if I played well I'd receive praises and attention.

Moving on and to escape living in Adelaide, South Australia, for no real reason other than I needed a job, playing hockey wasn't going to pay my bills, I joined the Air Force at 19. I was very naive in what that meant for a female, especially one entering into a male dominated trade. I quickly became surrounded by men and not ordinary men, men with massive egos. These ego's never lessened in my 22 years serving, they just changed form and got more cunning. But as I did with most things I saw this as a challenge and worked harder and smarter, usually longer but it paid off. Opportunities and promotions always found their way to me.

A new perspective

After my first mass awakening I began to see the world in a different light. My job, my marriage and my future purpose. Every week I was experiencing new elements of the spiritual world, forming a deeper connection with myself and discovering that I wasn't happy, and that I was really living in hell. There was no joy in my life. I was working full time, running a household with two children and trying to save a marriage. My then husband didn't want a bar of my spiritual experiences and I felt like I was split in two. There's only so many times you can be told 'that's how I am, I'm never going to change', before you stop communicating. I was filled with anger and rage because I couldn't express who I really was. I couldn't be my true self. That frustration was being directed towards my children and I knew that wasn't a life I wanted to live anymore or subject my kids to.

For the first time in my life I put my needs and the needs of my children first. I decided to leave my marriage. It then took 3 years to step out of the door as my logical brain needed to ensure I had done everything I could to rectify it. The time came and the axe was dropped. A period of pure chaos followed, and a husband in denial. It also meant a new job, moving to Canberra from Port Stephens, new house on my own and new school for my kids, all moving away from family support. I clearly don't do things in halves.

Time for change

You may think that going through a divorce with young children and finding my feet on my own, or serving in Defence for 22 years, are the most challenging things I have done. Far from it. The next 6 years I went into a preparation boot camp so to speak, getting me ready for my Divine Higher Self to come into my human form. That may sound a little far fetched for some of you but let me explain.

I said right at the beginning, to fully step into the light you must understand the dark. I was taken into the darkest elements of myself, many that I didn't even know existed. You know all those judgements you have on others? The negative thoughts you have about colleagues and your annoying family and friends? Well I was forced by situations and events to dive deeply into each of those judgments but about myself. Every lower aspect of myself was forced to come to the surface as my body and mind was continuously brought up to hold higher levels of light. This took its toll on my body, chronic fatigue, unexplainable illnesses and massive guilt because I wasn't able to work. You see, I believed that I was irreplaceable at work and that the world would stop rotating if I wasn't there. If I wasn't seen doing my job I wouldn't get promoted. Which was just a load of hogwash because the universe always had my back.

It was these beliefs that had me stuck in my job, I thought I mattered to the bigger organisation. At the end of the day I was just a number. I sat at my desk in my home office during lockdown, staring at the computer screen. My arms felt like lead and it took every ounce of my strength to log on. My body wanted to melt onto the floor and sleep for a month. The next day I submitted my discharge paperwork. I was done for good and the taste of freedom was so invigorating.

By living in the dark and working my way through it I was now on my way to experiencing the complete opposite, the light, and a lot of it.

No fear, only growth

I was 42 years old, a single mum, had never run a business and there I was registering my new company. Fear of the unknown, fear of being visible and fear of not making it were constant. Then I remembered my conversation with my 15 year old self. The fear began to melt away, the deep knowing that everything would work out was present.

This period of my life was when the real work began. Whilst still doing much transformational work over the years my guides and the greater universe had me sitting in survival mode. I was about to be accelerated into full transformation mode.

AN ENLIGHTENED *Life*

Every belief system, value, thought process, human program, everything that made me me was about to be tested under the universal microscope of humility. Light, dark, good, bad, up, down, high vibration, low vibration, every element of my ego was going to be assessed, broken down and released. Was I happy with this? One hundred percent, because it was my path. The best part about this was that I wasn't doing this on my own, my best friend and evolution buddy was walking the very same path of awakening. We supported each other from opposite ends of Australia. My next best support was my business. I had begun teaching all things spiritual and energetic to an amazing group of individuals from all walks of life and all across the country.

I completely accepted who I was to become and at this point I still didn't know who that really was. Whatever the end state, I was ok with it. I was on a path of discovery. Discovering my true self. Whilst doing this downloads of information regularly entered my body, some wiping me out for days others leaving me in a state of bliss, but all moving me forward.

Old aspects of self began to fade away and a stronger, happier, connected and balanced me emerged. It was at this point my Divine Higher Self began the process of entering my human form, beginning with the layers of my field and eventually my physical body and my brain. This process from beginning to end took over two years. The most difficult being when she entered my physical body and then my brain. I am at present still blending with her. Her name is Saramatu. Larissa has left the body. That is another story and really a book on its own. It was a process called live incarnation, it is an energetic passing of one soul energy and the birth of another all whilst the physical body is alive and well.

Larissa Beattie

Living with the new me

A sense of pure peace and calm lived within me whilst chaos and extreme exhaustion filled my days and the surface layers of my body. Internally I was connected to an endless stream of pure bliss. If I stopped long enough and breathed, focused inwards, my body would instantly relax, my mind emptied and I became one with my true self, Saramatu.

My struggles were with the patterns in my human brain and body. It had been functioning the same way for a very long time. Hardwired you could say. But with my new found inner vision and self observation I quickly identified the human programs that were running the show. With the assistance of the Divine, these programs were removed, some one at a time, others in bundles. I was becoming a blank canvas. Some might think that's the opportunity to create the you you've always wanted, but no, that's not what it is about. It's about remaining the blank canvas, that way you are living in a state of endless opportunities and infinite potential. That's what I am becoming. I am not completely there yet. Human elements creep back in, I observe them and then release them but it's not as simple as it sounds. I can at times get stuck in the human elements of living, running a business, and being a mother.

My ability to heal, transform and activate others was intensified beyond measure. What used to take an hour for me to do energetically with a client now took five minutes. People's lives were changing before their very eyes and mine. One of my skills at this time was my ability to very quickly awaken and connect individuals to elements of their highest self. It took me 12 years of hard work to connect to my Higher Self and now it was happening in a one hour session. It was blowing my mind.

AN ENLIGHTENED *Life*

You may be asking what exactly I do with my clients and students? That's a difficult question to answer as each person is different and no session is ever the same. On a broad scale, I feel, hear, see and know into people's energetic fields and body. Clearing out, repairing and upgrading all levels of self, physically, mentally and emotionally, past present and future. I open the access and activate individuals to step onto their highest path all whilst teaching them how to look after themselves energetically and be responsible for their own energetic evolution.

Who wouldn't want this? Everyone does. I was booked out solid three months in advance and was conducting close to 20 healings a week and teaching my students. This was a huge workload and not forgetting the prep work and clearing work required before and after each client. I was quickly headed towards burnout as I was giving way more than I was receiving. As a single mum with limited support, I was the only person that could give to me and I was exhausted. What did I do? I closed my books and took a break because I have learned that if I don't put my well-being first I can't help anybody else.

Time to expand and have mass impact

Life for me right now is in a state of flow, sometimes it is flowing upwards and sometimes flowing downward. Others may view this as turmoil but when you see everything as energy it is just a matter of moving that energy from one state to another.

How do I bring that into my human life? Well this is where my purpose comes into play. Remember I am here to do something big. My something big is to 'Awaken Humanity'. To deliver mass activations of awakening across the world, to crowds of hundreds of thousands of people. Opening them up to receive energy from higher consciousness.

2023 is the year where I step onto the global stage and step up to deliver what the Divine has blessed me to do. Expand your awareness, create a conscious world, and begin to heal Mother Earth. The beautiful thing is that I am not going to be doing this on my own. Masters from across the world will all come together and we will work together as one. When this happens we will be unstoppable and there will be massive radical change on this planet.

Approach each day with curiosity

Everyday I learn something new, it could be about humanity, the greater universe, the Divine or myself. When you choose to open your eyes and mind to learn, it naturally happens. Every day I wake up a new person. Everyday I am grateful for every experience I have ever had because it has all brought me to this point. A point of bliss and deep love for myself, that when I am truly connected, flows through me, it is me and I feel completely at one with all that is. I have no questions in this state. I have no worries or stress in this state. Everything flows around me and I become the observer. No judgement, I just am.

You may be wondering how you can have some of this. You can. It all starts with the want, need and desire to be the best version of yourself. And I don't mean by doing an online course or reading a self help book. I mean by observing the parts of yourself that don't serve you, or serve those around you. If it doesn't serve you in a positive way, work on it and let it go. By releasing the parts of you that no longer serve your highest good you discover the real you underneath.

The real you is pure bliss and is waiting patiently inside of you right now for it's time to shine.

AN ENLIGHTENED *Life*

How can you begin or accelerate your spiritual path?

It all starts with the foundations and all my students and clients, no matter what their experience level or knowledge, begin at the same place.

1. Get your shoes off and connect with the earth every day. If you can't take your shoes off then literally hug a tree. Minimum five minutes but twenty is best. There's a whole lot of scientific research explaining the benefits of Grounding.

2. Meditate daily in whatever form is best for you. Guided meditation, mantra, breathwork, exercise, whatever gets you out of your head, brings you into the present and connects you with your body.

3. Learn how to build light and hold light in your physical body. It's as simple as visualising a ball of white light in your chest. Intensifying that light and expanding it through your entire body. This will assist in balancing and feeding the body's energy systems, assisting it to heal faster and slow down the body's ageing system.

4. Accept that your EGO is going to do everything in its power to stop you from moving forward. It's even going to tell you that you don't have an EGO and that you're all good. Step out of denial. Everybody has work to do.

5. Find yourself a spiritual teacher. One that introduces themselves with their heart, not their list of credentials or accomplishments. If they don't resonate with you then don't be afraid to walk away. There is a right teacher for everyone and sometimes there is more than one. Listen to your heart and body and go with what feels right.

Larissa Beattie

"Life's not about living in survival mode. It's about doing what you love and loving what you're doing."

In love and light,

Saramatu

Larissa Beattie

Larissa Beattie also known as Saramatu is an Awakened Master, New Earth Leader, Multidimensional Trance Channel, Reiki Master, Mentor and Coach.

Leaving the Defence Force after 22 years Larissa stepped into her highest purpose and 'live' incarnated her Divine Higher Self, Saramatu.

Saramatu's purpose is to Awaken Humanity, New Earth leaders, lightworkers, healers and energy workers to step up to the next level of their spiritual evolution and fully awaken to their highest potential.

Her clients say:

"This program has been mind blowing. I was searching for so long to have this deep connection with self and have a deeper understanding of my spiritual journey. This program has been all of that and more..." Angela Mastrocinque

"I have learnt so many tools and techniques, but most importantly the discipline and routine in using them daily. I have shed many limiting beliefs, stories, patterns and aspects of myself, each making way for my higher self to shine through..." Anthony Hudson

Larissa is the CEO of Point of Presense a company she founded in 2020 where she runs successful live online workshops and programs. These programs are designed to work with any spiritual or healing modality and life in general.

'Infinite Potential' - live online 10 week program that focuses on expanding your level of consciousness and becoming responsible for your energetic body.

'Awakening Masters' - a 12 month intensive and acceleration program that transforms all aspects of life leading to a fully embodied awakened self, connected to higher consciousness.

Larissa is currently in the process of building an online Academy of Light (name will change), to store and deliver her teachings and the teachings of other Masters, to the global audience.

Website: www.saramatu.com
Facebook: www.facebook.com/SaramatuAwaken
Instagram: www.instagram.com/saramatuawaken
YouTube: youtube.com/channel/UCelAe2adeKX5wuX9qVbvLgg

Lisa Ohtaras

Energy Healer, Soul Healer, Intuitive Spiritual Coach, Spiritual Educator, Reiki Master, Seichim Master, Angelic Healing, Soulful Forgiveness® Practitioner & Workshop Facilitator & Author - Australia

CHAPTER 5

Lisa Ohtaras

An enlightened perspective of wounds

"Everything happens for a reason, a purpose, or for a lesson." ~ Lisa Ohtaras.

To all of the Light Beings Ascended Masters, The Divine and my Higher Self, I am eternally grateful for your education, guidance, unconditional love, support, spiritual gifts, and the work I have the privilege and honour to conduct.

Thank you to all my family, friends, affiliates, soul sisters, soul brothers, and clients who have assisted me on my spiritual journey to date. I am incredibly grateful!

Lisa Ohtaras

Over 25 years ago I became seriously health challenged and was blessed with the life-changing awareness that I was more than my name, personality, nationality, and religion. The spiritual awakening that followed changed my life.

I appeared to have it all in the physical world. I married the man I fell in love with, had two beautiful children, a supportive wonderful family, the dream home, and worked my passion as a registered nurse. Then halfway into my married life, my life fell apart.

I was diagnosed with the warning signs of Multiple Sclerosis. I had numbness that alternated with pins and needles, in my hands, arms, feet and limbs, pain in other parts of my body, hair loss, insomnia, night sweats, chronic fatigue and I could not then see clearly. Without this health challenge, I do not think I would have made the connection with my spirituality.

My naturopath prescribed vitamins, and supplements and instructed me to rest. However, after following this regimen to the letter I was told on my second visit that my condition had become worse instead of improving. This was another gift I was given, which propelled me deeper onto my spiritual path.

My spiritual journey and subsequent enlightenment showed me first-hand the Soul creates illness(es). Just as the energy is created, the Soul will uncreate it. With inner work, personal and Spiritual growth, and consistent meditation, and without the use of any medication, I healed myself from MS warning signs within two years.

I have a deep awareness and clarity today that my illness was one of the many great gifts I was given by my Soul. I would not be doing the Sacred work I conduct today, living and fulfilling my Sacred Contract, assisting people at Soul level where things are created, had I not done all the inner work and Spiritual growth, that I continue to this day.

Inner work became a dominant part of my life during and following my illness and is a consistent part of my daily routine. It has been a journey of constant enlightenment. Realising and understanding there were broader, wiser parts of me that were creating everything that was happening for me and not to me was one of the many revelations made to me from my Soul.

The Soul, the inner beings, and the collective consciousness from all of your lifetimes, are recreating their past life timelines during this incarnation so you can feel it to heal it.

A person's victim consciousness comes from within. Without inner work, the energy tends to persistently resurface.

Ignoring situations or circumstances, and even worse being in denial about things, creates an imbalance that can lead to health challenges, major illnesses, inner turmoil, and much more unfavourable energy.

Part of the human experience of being born onto planet Earth incorporates doing the inner work. Many people will choose not to and that is okay. It is a person's personal choice and free will that determines whether or not inner work is done.

Healing from within has many positive benefits. Healing the Soul helps the inner beings, and in turn, you to be more peaceful and helps expand their consciousness. Furthermore, inner healing helps the person to become aware, live from a conscious state of being, connect with their Soul purpose, Sacred contract, and make a positive difference to humanity, the animal kingdom, planet Earth, and/or the spirit world.

Inner peace and happiness can be attainable, by acknowledging what exists instead of ignoring or denying situations and then owning the good, not-so-good, and very unpleasant parts of yourself that have co-created in that event. Embracing your shadow and disowned parts and learning to forgive yourself and others is challenging, but emotionally freeing and empowering.

We are all one. There is no separation. That is an illusion.

When things in one's life are not progressing so favourably, know that there are daily opportunities being presented and created by the Soul to help one another.

Individuals in the world are an extension of some part of you, they reflect some part of you, and you reflect them.

When you find yourself being triggered by another person, it's a very conscious act to go within and recognise why you're being triggered in that way, is there a disowned part of yourself or suppressed event that needs acknowledging and releasing?

Acknowledging and releasing grievances, pain and trauma frees the Soul.

Sitting too long in the pain of past experiences keeps a person hostage to the emotions endured and the consciousness of the past. It is unproductive energy and why releasing that energy is a critical part of growth.

AN ENLIGHTENED *Life*

Negative emotions and a negative mindset can contribute to health challenges, and the subsequent formation of illness(es).

Your body is the barometer of your Soul.

Thoughts are very powerful. The human physical body is magnificent. It was created in a way so we could heal from within. When one holds a negative thought or belief, negative energy is created. Conversely, when one has positive thoughts and beliefs, a person has greater clarity, higher energy levels, feels happier, is more productive, is healthier, and more. The universe responds favourably to positive thoughts and positive energies by the Law of Attraction. Like attracts like. Amazing opportunities can come forth and doors that were closed in the past can open, for fruitful opportunities.

You have the power within you to change your thoughts at any moment. Be kind, gentle, and compassionate towards yourself and others. Avoid allowing world events to make you hard, and avoid holding onto anger as it leads to pain in your physical body.

The Soul is constantly giving us signals whenever there is an imbalance in one's physical body. Suppressed emotions can lead to health challenges, as I personally experienced over 25 years ago creating the warning signs of the autoimmune disease Multiple Sclerosis.

Begin each day with conscious intentions and in high vibration.

Every morning when I wake up, I always give gratitude to the universe and the Divine for the opportunity to be on planet Earth for another day, and for the blessings in my life that I'm extremely grateful for. I take nothing in my life for granted. It is a privilege and honour to be living during this current incarnation, with an abundance of daily opportunities to help heal my Soul and my spirit. Healing my Soul is of great importance to me as it helps me to find balance and peace.

Every morning I start my day by saying the following out loud:

Morning Affirmation©

I create & attract

GOOD HIGH ENERGY

GOOD HIGH ENERGY

GOOD HIGH ENERGY

I am the creator and attractor of

GOOD HIGH-ILLUMINATING ENERGY *and*

I HAVE VIBRANT ENERGY

to serve and support me today.

I received the affirmation during meditation many years ago and I recite it daily. The combination of words has a beneficial effect on my energy and the energy I receive from others.

I give one hundred percent of my attention to whatever I am attending to or doing.

AN ENLIGHTENED *Life*

Throughout the day, I am mindful of my thoughts that relate to me or others. If a negative thought surfaces from within me, I immediately acknowledge it exists and let it go. I release it from my consciousness and energy field, transmuting the energy and vibration into love and light and return it back to Source to the point of creation where it originated. Then I give gratitude to my Higher Self for the experience.

Throughout the day, I regularly pause what I am doing and sit quietly for a few minutes. My intention is to let go of and expel any energy through my breath, which does not positively serve me. I take a deep breath into the base of my abdominal area and hold the breath for a few seconds, then exhale. This process is repeated several times. It helps me to stay grounded, have clarity and be very focused on the work I'm doing.

If a problem or challenge arises or exists, I seek the SOUL-U-TION from within me. My Soul always has the answer most suitable for me. I immediately acknowledge the situation, let it go, forgive myself and the other person or people who co-created with me for the experience, and release the energy from my consciousness and energy field. The outcome is emotional freedom, inner peace and feeling empowered. I focus my thoughts and energy on things that bring me inner peace, and I consciously try to avoid energy that causes disruption to my inner peace.

Holding onto negative thoughts and emotions holds no positive purpose.

My Soul guided me to fall in love with myself a few years ago as I will always be with myself. Without the inner work that would not have been possible. I love and have embraced all parts of myself. It is an emotionally freeing and empowering feeling.

Whenever I make a mistake, I realise mistakes are necessary for the healing of my mind, body, spirit and Soul. Mistakes are created by design by my Soul and serve me a great purpose. When I learn the lesson or see the growth opportunity, I have transmuted the energy and my Soul rejoices.

I have learned to be gentle, kind, and understanding of myself as my Soul is recreating their past lives through my spirit this lifetime, which enables me to heal my inner beings and expand their consciousness.

Prior to doing deep inner work, I used to be judgemental of myself. That judgement was projected onto other people as that is the nature of the Soul. Judgement of others often comes from the Soul, an inner being or inner beings (who you have been in past incarnations). Following many years of inner work, which took time, money investment, energy, courage and commitment, I no longer judge myself for mistakes I have made in the past, or things I'd once wished I'd done differently. No person on planet Earth is perfect. We are all here to learn, grow, heal from within, change and evolve.

The Soul rejoices and celebrates whenever the inner work is done.

The level of Sacred work I'm doing would not have been possible had I not done the inner work during the past two and a half decades. The Divine informed me that as I have evolved, so has the depth and quality of work I conduct to assist people who are at crossroads in their life or experiencing challenges.

AN ENLIGHTENED *Life*

Working with clients at a Soul level is very Sacred work that I have the privilege and honour to conduct.

The Soulful Forgiveness ® & Atonement, Soul healing and Energetic healing work I conduct are transformative for clients. Through profound shifts in energy, people are able to forgive themselves and others who have caused hurt, harm, abuse, betrayal and more and have inner peace.

I have permission to share the following story. Very recently a client experienced a profound shift in her consciousness and energy field during the Soulful Forgiveness® & Atonement and Energetic healing session. At the beginning of each session, I ask my clients to rate the negative charge they have around the specific person and situation. The fifty-year-old lady was at a Number 10 (the highest level of negative charge) relating to two males she let go of, forgave, and released during the session. At the end of the energy healing process when I asked the lady what number she was now at, she replied "There is nothing there." She was feeling at peace relating to both males. I frequently witness this type of result.

I also have permission to share this story from a lady who has now passed, but who encouraged me to share her story to help others. I was informed of a lady, over 60 years of age, with terminal metastatic cancer (cancer throughout her physical body). Although she was very familiar with energy healing throughout her life, she'd been holding onto grievances and events that she could not shift or let go of. I began to work with her remotely, and after only a few sessions together, she said she had never experienced such inner peace and emotional freedom. I continued to do more work for the lady prior to her departure as a physical being from planet Earth, so she could be in total peace relating to all the people she had grievances with. She was so humbled and extremely grateful and able to transition to the spirit world peacefully where she is now at peace.

Soulful Forgiveness ® & Atonement and Soulful Self Forgiveness/Self Acceptance & Atonement is what I have been Divinely trained and prepared for during the past twenty years since I began Caring Energetic Healing. It is private work for the client, gentle, non-invasive, freeing people at the Soul level.

My Sacred mission is to help people who want to have emotional freedom at a Soul level freeing the Soul. I have been shown this repeatedly. The transformation of energy is amazing. I witness amazing results the majority of the time, whenever I conduct the Sacred work, seeing people feel at peace with situations that have been distressing them. Some people have carried the emotional wounding throughout many years and even decades of their life and via the deep Sacred work I facilitate healing the Soul, people are freed from the energy, resulting in emotional freedom and inner peace.

Results of course will vary according to the individual as every person is unique. However, frequently seen are transformative results such as inner peace and emotional freedom.

I also intuitively assist people through my SOUL-U-TIONS Coaching, to guide those seeking an enlightened path, to help people to have the understanding and awareness of why things have been created for them, what the significance is for them and their Souls, the growth opportunities being presented, why illnesses are present and the significance for the person and more.

AN ENLIGHTENED *Life*

My parting gift...

I want to share with you the beneficial wisdom which has helped me on my spiritual journey and Soul evolution, and I hope it will help you too...

1. Fall in love with yourself. People will come and go throughout your life, but you will always be with you.

2. Be true to yourself and align yourself with truth, and integrity and be authentic. Your spirit will soar to new heights and your Soul will rejoice.

3. Remember the power of forgiveness. Your Soul rejoices whenever you let go of, and forgive other people and yourself for things you are not at peace with. No one is perfect and we are here on planet Earth to learn, grow, heal, change and evolve.

4. Everyone is experiencing internal disruption they often do not speak about. Being kind and treating people respectfully brings forth positive energy for you and the other person or people. A simple word or gesture of kindness can make a major difference to a person's day and sometimes their life.

5. Live your life with an attitude of gratitude. All experiences serve a purpose. When you experience positive energy, always be grateful and know there is a growth opportunity or lesson with all unpleasant experiences for your awareness, growth, inner healing, and evolution of your spirit and Soul.

> "Go within, your Soul is waiting to speak."
> - Lisa Ohtaras

Infinite blessings,

Lisa Ohtaras

Lisa Ohtaras

Caring Energetic Healing

Lisa Ohtaras is a Best Selling Author, renowned Energy Healer, Soul Healer, Intuitive Spiritual Coach, Spiritual Educator, Reiki Master, Seichim Master, Medium, Channel, Soulful Forgiveness & Self Forgiveness/Self-Acceptance & Atonement Practitioner & Workshop Facilitator.

Over two and a half decades ago, Lisa healed herself of Multiple Sclerosis (MS) warning signs. Her diagnosis initiated an awakening from her Spiritual slumber and connected Lisa to her inner self.

Lisa transformed pain, numbness alternating with pins and needles in her hands and arms, feet and limbs, night sweats, insomnia, chronic fatigue, and visual challenges, all without medication.

Through her Spiritual connection, consistent daily meditation, personal growth, Spiritual growth and development, Lisa restored balance, harmony, and well-being to her physical body and emotional state.

Following Lisa's self-healing, she continued to work in her nursing career which collectively spanned over two decades. Then in 2003, Lisa commenced living her Soul Purpose Sacred Contract, and has been helping people with physical and life challenges, emotional matters of the heart and forgiveness challenges to living in balance, harmony, health, and the greatest version of themselves.

Website: www.caringenergetichealing.com
Facebook: www.facebook.com/lisaohtaras
Instagram: www.instagram.com/lisaohtaras
Linkedin: www.linkedin.com/in/lisaohtaras

Marika Gare

International best-selling author, International multi-award winner, Business Operational Management Specialist, Mentor, founder and Director of Perth Virtual Services and Women's Circle Facilitator - Australia

CHAPTER 6

Marika Gare

Journey to enlightenment

"Enlightenment is when a wave realises it is the ocean."

I dedicate this book to my Gran, always in my heart xx

I've been on a spiritual path most of my life, but it has only been after many challenges and coming into middle age that I truly understand what it means to live a fulfilling and enlightened life.

Being enlightened is to have an awakened understanding of yourself and of your journey in this life and beyond. To have joy in your heart and peace in your soul, being truly happy.

I have experienced many things during my lifetime that have placed me where I am today, but it is only through life's challenges and experiences that I have come to my greatest understanding.

When I was 2 years old, I fell off the back of a moving boat in Fremantle Harbour. My sister and I were fighting over some chips and in our struggle, I stumbled and fell backwards overboard. I remember being fascinated by the beautiful world I saw under the water, fish swimming about and a stray bit of green seaweed on the bottom. Just as I was about to plonk on to the sand at the bottom, there was a big splash above me and my dad came diving in fully clothed to save me. He grabbed my arm and swiftly brought me back up. I did not take a breath under water thankfully, so I was quite alright. Apart from giving my parents a monumental scare, but I was not in the slightest bit scared. It was just so beautiful and peaceful under the water.

That was my first brush with potentially losing my life.

When I was fourteen, I got incredibly sick incredibly quickly and spent months in and out of hospital, sometimes spending weeks in bed so sick I could barely get up and I was in excruciating pain every day. I saw multiple Dr's who had no idea what was wrong with me. Eventually, 8 months later I saw a child Gastroenterologist who diagnosed me with Crohn's disease. Crohn's disease is rare in someone so young and at fourteen I was told I would likely be sick like this the majority of my life; I would find it hard to hold down a job being sick all the time, I might find it hard to have a relationship and the chances of me having children were very minimal to nil. It was a lot to take in at such a young age and I became very depressed and wondered why this had happened to me. What was the point of my life? What had I done to deserve this? All my dreams were shattered.

AN ENLIGHTENED *Life*

About a month later I went in for emergency bowel resection surgery, the medication had not worked, and my organs were beginning to shut down due to malnutrition. I was only about 32kgs and if they didn't operate, I would die.

During the surgery my body was under so much stress, and I lost so much blood that I died on the operating theatre, they had to resuscitate me. Apparently, it was less than a minute that I flatlined but still not a great situation. I remember when I came out of theatre and they were wheeling me back to the ICU ward, my whole family was there. They had been given the call to come and see me as I wasn't expected to last the night, it was touch and go.

After a week in ICU I improved and was moved to a room I shared with a 10-year-old girl who was so happy to see me and have a friend to talk to. She was always playing happily and at my bed asking me questions and trying to have a conversation with me. I was feeling miserable and not really in the mood for conversation, I just wanted to wallow in my own misery. The nurses told me she had late-stage cancer and only a few weeks likely left to live. She was living the last of her days in hospital. So heartbreaking. I decided at that moment if she could be that happy knowing she was going to die and being so sick from chemo every day, who was I to be miserable in my recovery.

It was mid October 1992, and my team of Dr's advised me that I needed to prepare to be in hospital for the next few months recovering and that I'd likely be in for Christmas. I was not going to accept that, and I worked hard every day to try and get out of bed and to stand up and take a few steps. I was very wonky on my feet, had 3 drip trolleys attached to me which I needed to bring alongside with me as I walked, and I was in so much pain. Just walking 3 metres and back literally took me over an hour and utterly exhausted me. But I persevered.

Another 10 days later I walked out of that hospital. It took me a long time to walk out but I refused a wheelchair. The nurses cheered me as I left, knowing how much it took me to get to that point. My surgeon was amazed and could not believe how quickly I had recovered.

That was my second brush with death.

Three months after my operation, while I was on holiday with my friend and her family, my grandfather passed away after complications with heart surgery. One month after that, my other grandfather passed away from cancer. Two of my favourite people left this world and I missed them terribly.

At 22 years of age I had my first miscarriage, at 23 I had another miscarriage. Both were quite traumatic for me.

At 26 years of age my brother passed away and my family as I knew it fell apart. At 27 my beloved Gran passed away and during the same time my uncle also passed. A couple of years later my grandmother passed, just shy of her 100th birthday. So many significant people in my life gone.

At 34 I had a major car accident where we hit a tree and rolled the car several times. I was unconscious for around 40 minutes and suffered a torn spleen, bleeding on the brain, severe head trauma, a fractured skull and multiple deep lesions on my face requiring immediate plastic surgery. I lost 70% of my memory and damaged my vestibular system which gives you your balance, so I had a year and a half of physical and mental rehab, and it took a full 3 years for my brain to get back to full capacity again. It was a very long and difficult road.

This was my third and almost fatal dash with death.

AN ENLIGHTENED *Life*

During my extended recovery and rehab, my 12-year relationship broke down, I watched my father suffer multiple brain tumours and battle his own dance with death and intense rehab, and I somehow in my vulnerable state, ended up in a very violent relationship. This was the final straw.

I spent years feeling like I was cursed, destined to live a life of misery as I had so many challenging times presented to me. Every time I would start to get ahead, something else happened. I had lost so many beloved family members, and with that, lost their support and encouragement they always gave me, so it brought feelings of being lost in the ether, not knowing which direction to go.

I used to punish myself for negative situations in my life like it was my fault, and I was not worthy of anything else, but I was so young when many of these challenges came before me, I didn't know how to navigate through it all, so I blamed myself. It's hard to see through the darkness sometimes.

Eventually I sucked it up, blocked it out and carried on.

I know now that what I have endured in my life is my destined journey. I have endured these things for a reason, I have come out stronger and wiser and more determined than ever.

I now have the opportunity to share my journey and provides tools and guidance to those who are, or who have, struggled through situations in their life.

This is my true purpose and passion, to help and guide others in life, this is what brings me joy.

I have spent many years reflecting on my path, delving into my subconscious, learning my true purpose, finding peace within myself and embracing all that I am.

I must admit, it was only when I suffered my severe head trauma during my car accident and had an out of body near death experience that I really began my path to true enlightenment. I struggled for a long time to understand why it had happened after so many other negative experiences in my life and why I was encouraged to come back and complete my life when I had such incredible physical and mental challenges I needed to overcome. I wasn't good to anyone in the state I was in with constant pain and severe PTSD.

Losing so much of my memory, struggling with speech and my own confused thoughts, I had no choice but to build myself from the ground up again. To delve into my inner soul and make sense of what I had been through and the scattered bits of memories that began to come through over time.

As the memories came back, it gave me the opportunity to reflect and process them all over again, but without the emotional attachment that had occurred at the time it happened. Rather, I used the opportunity to understand how I felt during those times, how I reacted to situations and how it may have affected me moving forward. It was truly enlightening to view it from as distant perspective and brought great understanding for me.

Your memories are what shape you as a person, where you discover who you are, how you think, feel and act and how you process new challenges. Our minds are constantly utilising our past experiences to try and process and make sense of all that is happening around us. So if we have experienced negative situations or traumas that have significantly impacted us, it trains our brain to take hold of situations and create negative potentials in future situations. It is here where we need to retrain our brain again to see the positives instead.

AN ENLIGHTENED *Life*

We all have experiences that place us at our limit and that develop common patterns of anxiety and negative thought processes. One of the greatest challenges to overcome is yourself and your own inner critic.

I discovered through my reflection that the negative emotions I carried with me through the years were no longer serving me, and I began a process of internally restructuring my mindset and thought process. I learnt to honour myself and my emotions, to be kind to my inner soul, knowing I did the best I could at each stage of my journey, and I learnt what I needed to at that time, but it was now time to let go of the past and move forward with forgiveness in my heart to bigger and better things.

I used meditation as a special place to connect with my inner self and I learnt to transcend from my past into a greater place of wellbeing and enjoyment. I challenged myself and found gratitude for my experiences, for all that I am and where I was in my life.

I began to discover my life's purpose, to build my confidence again and to understand my gifts and how to truly love them and use them as was intended.

I embraced my life's journey and obtained a sense of connection and freedom that has brought so much happiness. It is now my mission to share this with others, particularly women, and reignite their purpose and passion for life again. It's so important to understand and love your journey and do what sets your soul on fire. We are here for such a short time so to learn how to grow and build and love your soul is the greatest gift you can give yourself.

By understanding and becoming aware of your life path, your true self, your true purpose and embracing all that has been your journey, you obtain such a sense of freedom and happiness, that it really is wonderful.

The road to enlightenment can be a challenging journey to begin, to reassess all that has been and your perception on each moment in your life, the crumbling away of untruths, seeing through the façade of pretence and is, in some ways, a complete eradication of everything you thought to be true.

It's a process that leads to a greater understanding and sense of self, of pride in all that you are and all that you do and confidence to move forward with greater insight, knowledge, and wisdom.

Reconnecting with challenging stages of your journey to observe the patterns and see how you grew at that moment, what responses you had as your younger self and what you might still hold on to that doesn't serve where you are now. You learn to focus on what your soul needs for your future happiness, what emotions you can let go of and what mindset serves you now.

Finding the best way forward and a way to navigate through potential future challenges with ease and strength.

I find the best way to navigate through is to find the positive in each situation. Not to be positive all the time, we must honour our emotions and process these as they are all important parts of the journey. But rather, once you have given yourself time to feel what you need to, to process what you need to and cry for days if that's what you need (this is your body's way of increasing the natural happy drug in your brain so is just as important to help you through these times), then after this moment focus on what positive lesson you can learn about yourself from the experience and how you can grow from it.

AN ENLIGHTENED *Life*

Finding light in the shadows and learning to dance in the storm – that is true enlightenment.

To start the process of enlightenment you must be kind to yourself. Know that regardless of what you have been through in life, you are worthy, you are wonderful, and you are capable of anything you set your mind to. If you really want it and it's the right path you have chosen, it will come.

As we grow up from childhood, we go from being encouraged to do and be all we can be, to being told that we are not good enough, that we shouldn't chase our dreams, that we don't look pretty enough or skinny enough or any other thing that society throws at us. And then we turn inwards and punish ourselves by losing confidence in who we are and what we want out of life, and we often have feelings of guilt and shame and of not being good enough or loveable enough. We stop trying to be all we can be, and we settle for what makes us feel enough, for what others want us to be and what is the safe choice.

Often when we reach middle age, we realise that perhaps life isn't what we thought it would be, we are not in the relationship we thought we would have, we have lost ourselves trying to please others or perhaps in our deep desire to nurture others, we reach empty nest time and feel lost and confused. Who am I without work or children or a partner?

Trying to connect back with yourself and find your passion and purpose again is something you must give yourself permission to do, to follow your heart and dream again. To rediscover and nurture your true self and find what sets your soul on fire. Obtain the life you want for you, and you alone.

Today I am lucky enough to have all I dreamed of; I have worked hard to get where I am, but I have true happiness in my heart.

I understand my path and I accept it.

My dream for the future is to encourage people to find their true selves, to empower them and ignite their potential.

My Wisdom

Some little pieces of wisdom to start you on the journey:

Start a Journal – write down all your emotions of how you are feeling, where you are at in life, what you feel you are missing, what you would like to change and what brings you true joy in life. Writing helps to navigate and start the process. Understanding where you are at and reflecting on what you really want.

Heal Your Inner Soul – through mediation and guided practise. There are pathways to learn confidence, to feel good and be kind to yourself, to understand what you truly want out of life and to heal past traumas. Stop doubting yourself and step back into your power. Go find yourself again and know you will be ok no matter what the situation.

Find your Purpose – what is it that sets your soul on fire? What is your life passion? What's holding you back? Is there something you are running away from? Things don't always happen at the click of our fingers or go to plan. In fact it rarely does. But our own resistance to change is the most challenging. It forces us to make major changes and step out of our comfort zone. It is not always convenient or easy but know what the endgame is, take one step at a time and just start. When we

AN ENLIGHTENED *Life*

move towards our purpose and calling in life, our whole energy shifts and synchronicity begins to flow.

Honour your Vision – our own self-talk is the worst; we can be so hard on ourselves. I won't be good enough, what if it doesn't work, I can't change my life now and follow my dreams. Don't be stupid. What am I thinking? Stop listening to your inner critic who resists change. Listen to the other voice within, the positive one wanting more, knowing your worth and sharing your joy and excitement. This is your voice of truth, the one that honours your vision.

Change your Mindset – connect with others. Join a local community group of like-minded people who will support and empower you. Life is about making the right connections and having a village around you to support you. We are all going through this life together and we all share our desire to find our true selves and ultimately be truly happy in life.

> *"Be fearless in the pursuit of what sets your soul on fire".*

Marika Gare

Perth Virtual Services

Marika has over 25 years of experience working in small businesses and in State Government roles. She founded her own business Perth Virtual Services in 2019 after having her first child. Making the decision to follow her dreams and start her business provided flexibility to work around her son and live the best of both worlds.

Within 2 years, the business was both sought after and successful, winning multiple business awards both national and international. She became an internationally published author of multiple #1 best-selling books on business and personal development, became a certified women's circle facilitator, facilitated multiple workshops, and created a new business brand called Marika Gare - Be Inspired, which focuses on life coaching and inspiring others.

Marika is passionate in supporting women across the globe and has many collaborative projects with various organisations that help women achieve success in both business and life.

The inspiration behind her achievements is being able to help women from all backgrounds and experiences to be the best version of themselves, so they can exceed in life and have the confidence to chase their dreams.

Website:	www.marikagare.com
Email:	marika.inspire@gmail.com
Facebook:	facebook.com/marikagare.beinspired
LinkedIn:	www.linkedin.com/in/marikagare

Rosie Shalhoub

CEO & Founder of Embrace Australia - Sydney, Australia

CHAPTER 7

Rosie Shalhoub

Embracing magick

"Life happens when you least expect it and not getting what you want can be a blessing in disguise."

To the Universe, who knows what is best for me way before I do. For your infinite wisdom in every moment that always leads me to a life of happiness and fulfillment, and for the endless blessings which I accept with love and understanding.

According to the trusty Google search, 'empowerment' is the process of gaining control over your life and having the freedom to make decisions that serve you best. Well bloody hell, that sounds good, so I signed up for it. Actually, I lined up for years, I waited my turn slowly, slowly, whilst others pushed in front, stole, lied and downright played dirty. And yet, I still waited.

Not being a very patient person at the best of times, I surprise myself looking back at not only the patience I did have, and not knowing I had it, but the resilience and the never lacking belief of faith in God that yet someday my turn will come.

Growing up as an Australian-born Lebanese was not an easy feat back in the 70s and 80s. I never really knew what side of the coin I was placed on, so at some point in my teenage years, I decided that the edge of the coin was best. And so, my friends, I have lived on the edge ever since.

My dad was a strict Lebanese father, who loved his children with all of his heart and soul, and yet his life was always spent at work. Back in those days, immigrants tended to work in their own business, and my father was no different. He had a sharp business brain, and he knew how to make money. Dad also went for the fine things in life, so we never went without, and in a way, you could say I was spoilt. OK, I will say it... I WAS spoilt.

But when you live in a big fat Lebanese family, it is not only your parents who do the discipline, the decision making and the spoiling, it is the whole bloody family... grandfathers, grandmothers, aunties, uncles, cousins, and second cousins. Hell, we may as well throw in the next-door neighbours in there too, along with their cat!

As a mother myself, I understand that we want to give our kids everything, and we do it as our way of showing love, especially if your love language is the same as mine. I am so guilty of this, I am expecting one day in the not-too-distant future to be placed in the Hall of Fame as the world's most loving mother – who spoilt her kids!

AN ENLIGHTENED *Life*

However, being one step ahead than my parents were, I have become more conscious every day that now my twins are almost 17 that perhaps they can make their own bed, or do their own washing, or heck, even get themselves to the bus stop! (No heckling or berating here please other mums, it's my thing, OK?)

Out of my parents' love of wanting to give us everything we wanted, what they didn't realise, was that we weren't given the foundation of life, yet indeed we were given the unlimited energy of love and material possessions. Nobody told me back then that life was going to be hard, filled with heartbreak, sorrow, broken dreams, financial loss, disappointments, and a few marriages thrown in there to boot! And so, realising this as I write, and not wanting this shock for my children in years to come, I didn't make their lunch for school today!

I actually really believed that my prince charming was going to come along the way my dad did for my mother and sweep me off my feet where we lived happily ever after. That didn't happen. Instead, for some unknown psycho-analytical way, I had to become my very own prince charming. Ummmmm, I don't remember reading this in the fairy tales, the ones I became so accustomed to reading, each and every night. My prince in shining armour was to replace my father and look after me until eternity, and spoil me like a princess because back in those days I was one. Maybe only in my father's eyes, but one nonetheless.

And so, as I waited for Prince Charming, I found myself settling for the court jesters. One after one they came, and each time I also found myself supporting them!

I would find them like you would find 5 cent pieces on the ground, they were everywhere and just like a 5 cent piece useless too. I would pick them up, and put them in my pocket where they stayed until it was time to empty out my pockets.

Each one had a different face, but they all had the same story. All lost puppy dogs, looking for a woman to love and look after them, and somehow I became the one who had the balls in each relationship and yet, I was yearning for it to be the opposite way around.

Support came to them the only way I knew how, and that was what I learnt from my parents. I learnt that money and financial assistance equaled love. I was very much loved back by these men, but each relationship found me living on the edge of that bloody coin. It was fun, spontaneous, never boring, and oh full of drama. When it became quiet, I looked for more drama, and if I couldn't find it I made it.

Then it happened. All of the sudden there were no more 5 cent coins. Not one. Zilch. Nudda.

The last 5 cent I had ripped my heart out into pieces. It was the type of heartbreak that you would see in the movies, where the heroine's world gets flipped upside down and all she is left with are her feelings of sorry, emptiness, and rejection. That was me. I could no longer breathe, nor eat, in fact, I was just surviving. I moved back into my parents' home where I would, as a 28-year-old woman, curl up next to my dad in his protective, recognisable arms where I felt safe.

Unfathomable waves of an anguish had coursed through my body as I began to realise that nothing would ever be the same again. All the joy that I thought I had in that relationship, and all the passion that was just superficial, was suddenly gone in an instant. I had been heartbroken before, but not like this. Nobody told me it could hurt this much to have my heart broken and every day seemed like an unbearable maze of grief, despair, and darkness.

AN ENLIGHTENED *Life*

In never wanting to feel that pain ever again I started to find myself expressing my sorrows through art therapy. I found my niche in specialising in hand-painted glass ornaments and each day my heartache was being replaced with something exciting. Jumping out of bed to just paint my little backside off was fun until I realised that it wasn't going to pay the bills.

I found myself setting up stalls in markets across Sydney, then it became school fairs and local charity events until I ended up with my first pop-up shop in a Westfield shopping centre. And then it happened…. a customer asked me to write a name on a Christmas bauble she had just bought from another store, and the rest became history.

By the following Christmas, I had established myself as the woman with balls – literally! My Christmas balls business grew to a 7-figure business in which I only had to work 2.5 months of the year! I mean seriously? WTF? Within the first three years, I was making more in that short period of time than most people were working all year. With this new-found financial freedom, I found myself looking after myself, with a nip and a bit of tuck here and there, I looked good and that made me feel good.

I made my own money on my terms, and year after year, 'Santa's Little Painters' became a household name. Six years into the business I franchised it and then something happened… I went on what was to be a two-week holiday with my cousin to surprise visit my aunty and grandmother in Lebanon. I had never been to the country, and quite frankly, I was a single woman with not a care in the world. I had no man to answer to, no children to need me, and a business that gave me so much freedom that it was a no-brainer whether to go to the middle east or not.

Those two weeks lasted two weeks for my cousin, however, they lasted three years for me. As I said my goodbyes to her at the airport in Beirut, I walked back to the car and had never felt the overwhelming sense of freedom that I felt right at that very moment. I had no clue where I was going to stay, no idea how I was going to get around, and no concept of how to speak the language properly. I lost a lot of weight whilst there, partly because I lived on a Mediterranean diet, and the other part because I partied hard all through the night, dancing on table tops as they do there.

I hired myself a small chalet at the heart of the Mediterranean ocean in the city of Batroun which I think about every single day since I was last there in 2005. Batroun became my home, and it also became the birthright of my future twins. Laid bare amongst the ancient Phoenician rubbles, the town was refuge to a glorious beach, my room overlooked the ocean, and I was home.

I remember clearly sitting on my balcony one night talking to the full moon in all her glory, and I found myself thinking out loud. At one time, many years prior, the thought of breaking up with my partner seemed like the worst thing imaginable. But years later, sitting here as the waves sang in unison with my thoughts, I finally realised that not all endings are meant to be sad. If it weren't for that breakup, I would have never embarked on this journey of personal growth and development.

I encountered tough challenges along the way, but they only made me stronger and more determined than ever before. Looking back now, I can see how all of this heartache was a blessing in disguise – it gave me the freedom to pursue my passions and allowed me to be even more successful than if I had stayed in a broken relationship.

Even though I lived in Batroun for three years, I came back to Sydney every Christmas to run my Christmas shops. I was

AN ENLIGHTENED *Life*

able to set them up from the sidelines of the chalet pool over the phone or email, whilst wild Arabic dance music was playing out loud, a shisha pipe by my side (not that I ever used it, but it just sounds good for the purpose of this story), and a pool boy, who later came to be the father of my twins.

He arrived in Sydney on the day of the infamous Cronulla riots, which took place only a few minutes from where I lived. Either it was an omen or a sign, but the news of the riots travelled far and wide, as phone calls from Lebanon were coming back to us.

It was here that I found myself at the peak of my career. I was making money, I was an established household name within the community, and I was about to give birth to two extraordinary pigeon pair of twins, Joey and Ellie. So why did I feel so empty?

Needless to say, being married to an 'import' is not always a good thing, especially when your cultural difference collide, so within the first 12 months of Joey and Ellie's existence I became a single mother. I also became the exact opposite of who I wanted to be.

After the drama of telling my very conservative Lebanese family that I was pregnant with twins, which in Lebanese terms meant I was no longer a virgin (at 38 mind you), my mother started to pray the Hail Mary every single day after that. Now it was time to tell them that I had split with the father of their first grandchildren, a feat I wish on nobody ever! You see, when you are an adult in a big, fat Lebanese family you really never are one and I found myself converting back to a teenager all over again. However, the fear was worse than the actual bite and I packed up our bags and went to live with my parents once more. To be honest, I enjoyed being back there.

Rosie Shalhoub

It was time to visit my accountant who had encouraged me to keep up with the Santa's Little Painters franchise. I spent my days putting together franchise manuals, doing homework on other franchises, talking to lawyers, and creating a concept that came out of a fairy tale. There was only one problem and that problem was my accountant's wife. She took my concept from scratch to finish, my original artworks and designs, and my whole business structure and made it into her own. This time my heartbreak came in a different form, but it was no different from the first. I was still young and saw myself as a successful entrepreneur with dreams of taking my Christmas shops in to shopping centres all across the globe. And yes, I had an innovative spirit, and I knew it was a brilliant idea, but somebody else who had more money and clout than I, and no children I may add, also thought it was a good idea too.

Once again, I felt betrayed and helpless as I saw my idea being stolen from under my nose. For days I was in despair and rage at how someone who was meant to be a professional could do such a thing. I was enraged with fury every time my designs would pop up on Google under 'her' business name. With baby twins in tow and no financial help from their father, I was left with no choice than to waitress at my sister's café. I was still breastfeeding at the time, and looking back at how I made that work, I realise that I am a bloody superwoman I am! Lucky for me both my parents would come to the centre where I was working and take the twins for a stroll until I had finished my shift, so that took the edge off things a bit. I eventually came to terms with the situation of my stolen business and realized that the only way forward was to move on and put all of my energy into creating something even better. With determination and courage, I made it my mission to create something even more revolutionary than before, refusing to let this setback define who I was or stop me from achieving great things.

AN ENLIGHTENED *Life*

It was during a busy lunch break when I waitressed on a group of CEO's discussing a closed shop within the shopping centre and what they were going to do with it. As I leant in to hand over their coffees, in a cheeky voice I said "give it to me". Never in my wildest dreams did I think they would take me up on the idea and 'Embrace' was born!

We were the pioneers in the crystal industry, and our place became a well-known spiritual hub for people longing to find something in themselves but not knowing what. Our three psychic rooms were booked out day in and day out, we offered personalised service, and we became friends with our customers as we cried, laughed, and cried some more with them. We embraced everybody regardless of colour, race, religion, age or sexuality. So many lives were touched because of us, and so many hearts healed. Embrace was a beautiful environment that brought peace and harmony to all that visited. She also made me money too, and lots of it.

That was thirteen years ago now.

Two years later in walked the love of my life into Embrace. A very handsome Italian man, who became my rock and the prince charming I was looking for. The problem was I no longer needed a prince charming because I had already turned into him by looking after myself, doing it my way, and gaining independence on no one but myself . Ross came into my life as my equal and because I stopped looking for a prince, I didn't need one after all. Instead, what I found in him was a king. Together and twelve years on we are the perfect Brady Bunch and some days not so perfect, with six kids between us and a love that knows no bounds.

Embrace has had many facelifts during her time, but the biggest is about to get underway with the opening of the Embrace

Academy and with the help of my husband Ross who led me to the idea. It will be an online hub for spiritual entrepreneurs who really want to manifest some big things in their lives. I am excited about the next chapter, knowing that somewhere down the track we will face another hurdle to jump, taking us off in a different and more positive direction once again.

You see, not getting what you want can be a difficult pill to swallow at first. But if you look beyond the surface, it can be an opportunity for personal growth and discovery. Instead of letting yourself get stuck in disappointment, turn it into motivation to attain something even better. The disappointment of not getting what we want allows us to find new paths and explore different possibilities that we might never have considered before. It also encourages us to push our boundaries and strive for more than what we initially set out to achieve. In the end, not getting what you want may be just the thing you need to open your eyes and see the bigger picture, and it could be your biggest stroke of luck.

Sometimes the sliding doors are right in front of us, we just have to know how to open them.

Rosie Shalhoub

Rosie Shalhoub has been recognised as an inspirational entrepreneur, and the founder and CEO of Embrace, Australia's most loved crystal, spiritual and metaphysical store. She is also the founder of the wildly successful Santa's Little Painter's franchise.. She is literally the woman with "balls", both crystal ones and Christmas ones!

Rosie is an internationally acclaimed award winning and Amazon best selling author of THE DARK SIDE OF THE LIGHT, and THE CHOCOLATE LOVERS MESSAGE CARDS.. She has also been featured in The Huffington Post,and published in Successful Women in Business. Strong Women Finish Rich, The Wellbeing Book and The book of Inspiration for Women

With her husband Ross, she founded the "Festival of Dreams" a three year project at Sydney's Hordern Pavilion. It was here where Rosie found international recognition working alongside Hollywood movie stars, Native American chiefs, our countries Indigenous elders and well known inspirational speakers. The festival gathered over 100 exhibitors in the mind, body and spirit fields, with high profile speakers, 1000's of visitors and the most acclaimed spiritual & inspirational speakers from around the globe.

Embrace, Ross and Rosie joined forces in Embracing Rosie, a New York award winning, charming, funny and completely unscripted eight-part reality show. Embracing Rosie gave us all an insight into the life of Rosie, Ross, their family life and her beloved Embrace. She now runs THE STONED QUEEN podcast on Spotify.

Email: contact @embraceaustralia.com.au

CHAPTER 8

Sharon Le Fort

Standing strong

I dedicate my chapter to my children who were my anchors I needed in moments where life got pretty dark, and evoking memories of precious moments shared between us, gave me the strength to continue to survive. I love you with all my heart and soul.

I also dedicate this chapter to the forgotten survivors of childhood domestic and family violence and abuse.

Sharing our stories of not only survival also the potential impacts of abuse and violence we experienced, furthers the power of enormous post traumatic growth.

Sitting here out the back of my house, under the portable pergola, surrounded by potted palms, tinged by the harsh sun here in Queensland. Listening to the water trickling down the two miniature waterfalls, placed nearby. I've been pondering the question of 'what it means to live an enlightened life', examining whether I am in fact 'enlightened' or not.

To save me from going down the rabbit hole, I searched online for a definition which is something I do when my thoughts take me through a labyrinth.

As stated in a blog on: https://www.panachedesai.com/4-ways-to-live-in-enlightenment/

"When you learn to live in an enlightened state, you are relying on your own knowledge and experience to garner the direction you take in life. You don't rely on others to tell you your direction. You have confidence that what you choose to do, think, eat, have faith in…are all the right choices and decisions."

I smiled and said to myself 'YES, this is me… well, mainly me!'

Therefore, here I am, confident in the understanding, I, in fact have lived an enlightened life. It may not have felt that way at times, great to know I have been.

Now, that's all sorted.

Allow me to take some of your precious time and share with you my experience and wisdom. This has seen me move from victim-survivor of childhood domestic and sexual abuse to thriving-survivor, sharing the impact of witnessing, and experiencing horrific abuse including, non-fatal strangulation.

This will be a bit heavy at times, but please be reassured, I'm great now, I'm thriving and generally, not living in 'survival' mode.

AN ENLIGHTENED *Life*

I'm a woman with a mission to facilitate healing and guidance for those who are forgotten survivors of childhood domestic and family violence.

I have three beautiful and courageous children, two of which are adults making their mark in the world and the third is completing high school. I'm also a confidante to my ex-partner's children and 'Nanny Sharon' to their children, who I adore with my whole heart. My own daughter is having her first baby, a girl!

I keep pestering to find out the name they've chosen for our precious girl, however, my daughter is very closed-lipped. Even bribing her with different things won't pry those lips open.

I share a house with my ex-partner, who is dad to my youngest son. We get on (most of the time, anyway) . It works well with shared roles with our son, and it lowers the living costs; something we've all had to think about over the last few years.

We also have Walter, our big white and ginger furball of a cat who spends his day wondering what the hell is going on with our dachshund 'Penny', who loves chasing her tail or skidding across the tiled floor.

It wasn't always like this for me, especially growing up.

I never knew if anyone had experienced life like I had.

Unsure, when I would come out from under my bed or the bedroom cupboard, wondering would I discover my mum dead on the floor. With each step taken, not knowing if 'he' was going to come out and hurt me as well.

My earliest memory as a child is when I was around 8 years old, being hoisted up by my mother through the kitchen window, to unlock the back door. I remember being petrified and trying so hard to be quiet. I hopped down from the kitchen sink onto the floor, turning towards the laundry where the back door of the house was, only to find a chair had been placed in the doorway with glasses balancing on top of the edge of it, alerting 'him' if we had come back in the house. I climbed back up onto the sink letting mum, who was still outside, know about the glasses. She told me to go and unlock the sliding door in the lounge room. I remember feeling like my breath was caught in my chest, what if 'he' was in the lounge room? Was 'he' waiting....

I courageously went from the kitchen to the lounge room, poked my head around the corner to see if 'he' was there, no he wasn't, but their bedroom door was closed, though. I quickly walked/ran over to the sliding door and threw myself against my mum, who had my little brother with her.

I had never really allowed myself to reflect on that particular night whilst undergoing therapy, the reason being, to voice it verbally, it would have meant my inner child would have had to relive it. However, I did in time find a therapist who provided a nurturing space to heal what needed to be healed in each moment.

More about that soon.

Becoming aware of signs such as mood swings, playing with loose change in his pocket, the moon cycles, clapping of hands and many other traits, became the norm for me. I spent many afternoons and evenings on 'hyperalert'. Looking for any signs to indicate what kind of night we were going to endure.

Survival was exactly what it was, and to be very honest with you, it's a bloody miracle I did in fact, survive.

By the time I reached my teens, I had been seen as 'prey' for others' pleasures, such as isolated, having no parental protection, regularly left in cars outside pubs or as I got older left to my own devices, surrounded by adults who were under the influence of alcohol or drugs, or both.

By the time I reached fifteen years of age, I was raped by my boyfriend who was three years older.

I never had romantic fantasies of my 'first time', as the reality of my environment was that sex was always a by-product of nights fuelled by alcohol and violence.

Forced to drink cheap wine, my boyfriend, holding the glass to my mouth, coaxed me to lay back on the four-seater white retro vinyl backed lounge. With the word "NO" not heeded to; my head dizzy from the alcohol, my body losing the battle.

Not only had my boyfriend not given any thought to the impact of his actions on me, he also gave no thought to the person laying on the floor (him).

I got up from the lounge, walked past 'him' on the floor, gripping the wall to help me balance, I fought the urge to be sick whilst I walked past my younger brother with feelings of mortification and enormous shame, I went straight to the toilet and threw up.

When I got back to the lounge, my boyfriend got up and walked out and went home and that was that!

From that moment, there was a small nagging voice deep within my memories, always wondering if, 'he' was lying there awake and hearing everything or was HE asleep?

With what I know of 'him' now, it's more than a possibility 'he' was awake, as this was 'his' modus operandi. This was proven, by an event that happened around a year or so later when 'they' brought a 'friend' back home and this 'friend' had told 'him' I had flashed my vagina at him at the pub.

With being told of this blatant disgusting lie 'he' told me to get undressed and join them. I stood there as a 16-year-old being told by someone I was meant to trust and have their protection from this kind of behaviour. If I didn't get undressed and join them, I could get out of the house... I walked out of the house with the door being locked behind me!

Who does that?

At the age of eighteen, I left one war zone and moved into another. This time, it was with alcohol and sex. There is a dangerous line between 'exciting' and 'recklessness'.

I viewed sex as something that, if you don't do what is expected, there will be devastating consequences and although I was not living within that war zone any longer, the impact of the life I had prior, was firmly imprinted and, therefore, the warrior within turned the tables around and became the seeker.

I'm going to embrace my vulnerability here and introduce you to Shazz – my warrior within. The wild, crazy, 'I don't give a f*&k', part of me.

After a few years of therapy, I connected to what my therapist had been trying to convey to me from the beginning of our journey together. I have "dissociative identity disorder". Dissociation happens as a result of trauma and assists with keeping tough memories at bay. It's also a lot more complex than that but as a result, Shazz is one of my Alters and my warrior!

Seeking out men to fill a deep internal void, not realizing at that time in my life, it was never going to be satisfied regardless of how sexy, adventurous, hardened, or even caring, they were.

At times it never mattered to me, whether I'd see them again or not, as I was never without someone to have 'fun' with. Yet, when I was alone and sober, which was during the week, I would have this deep longing for something more, something deeper, something I knew I deserved.

While Shazz was a bit uncompromising at times, I wouldn't be here today, if it wasn't for her.

I've come to a point of acceptance and understanding of the moments where Shazz stood strong and basically took no crap from others and didn't say no to propositions of group sex, kink, and binge drinking. She said – 'Bring it'.

Shazz loves all things risqué, pushing those boundaries just a bit further each time. She has her own persona, she walks with an air of distinct confidence, she will make direct eye contact with the men who think they are being covert, she will swear like a trooper, turn the music up, and flirt up a storm, because she can.

She is, as a friend of mine named her fittingly 'Shazza Fierce'.

She also has an incredible inner warrior strength and a way of seeing exactly what's in front of her and will deal with it head on. Now, this was great when 'we' needed to 'survive' but in all honesty, it wasn't great in everyday life.

I would go from kind and compassionate to feisty and angry, almost like 'we' were ready to go into battle. When there was a perceived threat, Shazz would come in and before I knew it, it was different. 'I' would feel something had changed with no idea, in what way.

I would go from 'nice' to unfiltered. Even to this day, there are moments where she will just jump in with her two cents worth and tell it how it is.

Fast forward to my mid thirties, I was now divorced after a 14-year marriage to someone who I had put on a pedestal for too many years. Following him up and down the east coast of Australia for his career.

Throughout those years, Shazz appeared frequently. He would frequently tell me, "you are just like your family", that "you need to lose weight", "you are not thin/pretty/smart enough". Shazz would yell back "I'm not fucken who you say I am" or "stop fucking talking to me like that". Shazz would take it further and call him a fucken arsehole, or to shut the fuck up or worse.

The binge drinking had stopped before I had children, as I took motherhood very seriously and was very nurturing and affectionate with my two young children. However, that changed after divorce. Within a month or two of our separation, I was experiencing emotional and financial abuse from him. Leaving me to make the house repayments, after promising he would help, which resulted in me having to go bankrupt and lose our home. It wasn't long before I was back in 'survival' mode which saw maladaptive behaviours of drinking excessively and online chat rooms. Spending hours 'meeting' men who could provide an 'outlet'. I ventured into phone sex – convincing myself it was okay, I was home with my children, they're safe!

I acknowledge I wasn't the best mother at this stage, believing if I made sure their basic needs were met, I was being a 'good' Mum.

Until one day a few years down the track, I 'woke' up.

It was a day like today, sitting out the back of the house I was living in with my young daughter – (my eldest son was living with their father) feeling the desperation of needing to bring income into our house. I considered becoming a sex worker. I

AN ENLIGHTENED *Life*

thought, if I was expected to be this person, I should be earning money from it.

I sat, phone in hand, looking at a classified ad I'd seen in the paper. As I reached to dial, a small voice inside me became louder and louder saying.

"This is not you!"

After what felt like the longest thirty seconds, I put the phone down, got out a journal and pen, and asked some brutally honest questions,

- What the Fuck do you want in your life?
- How are you going to make it happen?
- When are you going to do it?

I wrote out my five-year plan, breaking it down into one year action steps. This was the *first* turning point.... Even though I was in a place of 'doing', I was still not connecting with the place of 'being'.

It would take at least another ten years before I connected to the essence of who I am.

Experiencing our 'breakthrough', at the age of fifty-one.

My mind and body said "enough," I could not continue in that place 'doing', which in this case, 'survival'.

I went to my doctor, with her nurturing manner, we went through a list of psychologists within the local area and came to agree on one.

I knew I was in safe hands with 'J' when at the very first appointment she said, "I'm here for the long haul". It's been over five years now.

Eight months into therapy, I connected, I was in fact a Survivor! It was also when I had understood all the sexualised behaviours I had witnessed and experienced as a child and adolescent were in fact sexual abuse/assault.

It was not 'normal' to have been around this kind of environment, being exposed to adult behaviours and abuse.

This insight gave me the clarity to appreciate what I had experienced during sex was in fact, dissociation.

When we weren't reaching those exhilarated orgasms, "Shazz" would lose her shit. Every time had to be paralleled to an 'out-of-body' experience, with the afterglow likened to lying in pillows of clouded euphoria.

I began to grasp how there are alternate parts of me which have their own unique needs, as well as distinct ways of expressing themselves.

This incredible insight has facilitated such extremely and enlightening post traumatic growth.

I started to remember how I used to practice self-care on Sunday nights with bubble baths, candles, a glass of wine and Gregorian chants. This ritual would prepare me for the next week, where I was working within the mental health sector at the time.

Other memories began to surface, in particular, how we would take a daytrip to Cronulla, Sydney, and I would visit a specific spiritual book shop, filled with candles and self-help books. It was the highlight for me as I felt I found a 'path'.

AN ENLIGHTENED *Life*

Living in 'survival mode' for so long, the feelings of immense joy I experienced in this shop had been completely blocked from my memories.

Healing those multi-layered traumatic events I've been able to unlock different aspects of my life and gradually the memories are returning, albeit a bit foggy, Nonetheless, I can now picture walking through the doorway of the shop; my senses alerted to the sweet perfume of the incense, the soft subtle tones of pan flutes (it was the 90's) and waterfalls playing in the background, and the bookcases lined around the room, filled with books written by authors sharing their insights, showing us how to move through shame and heal the toxicity we've been surrounded by.

This bookstore was an introduction to what I soon learnt as healing within.

I once thought, when you work through one area of your past, it goes back into its little box, no longer having power over you.

What I found though, is, healing is not a linear process. It's like a maze with squiggle lines going in all directions. Although, doubt sets in from time to time or feeling others know more or better than I do.

I always came back to the awareness that I am my own person and I know what is best for 'us' and I have learnt to listen to that voice within, 'my soul'. Understanding, I'm guided by my soul, and everything will be okay as long as I'm going with the 'flow'.

In saying this, it doesn't mean I don't get lost from time to time and allow the 'inner critic' to take up space in my thoughts.

Through, acknowledging how far I have come, from that petrified eight-year-old girl, climbing through the kitchen window, to the person I am today.

A woman, who has co-authored four books, built a transformational coaching business, partnered up with a domestic violence charity, providing vision board workshops for survivors, and saying YES to opportunities, like being a contributor to the 'She Simply Impacts' community.

Holding space for participants in the Emotional Support Group.

As I previously shared, my mission is to facilitate healing and guide forgotten survivors of childhood domestic and family abuse. It is also to de-stigmatize the impact of childhood domestic and family abuse, mental health, and dissociative identity disorder.

I will leave you with a very important message:

Find your inspiration, hold on to it, allow it to take you to those places you have always dreamt about. For that's living 'An Enlightened Life'.

"Stand strong in your truth, for it is your truth, and no one can take that from You."

Sharon Le Fort

Whether Sharon is working with individuals or groups, the result is often the same: new perspective, new insights, renewed vigour and changed outlook.

Sharon's background had seen her spending her entire childhood navigating a war zone of domestic abuse, fraught with physical, emotional, and inappropriate sexualised behaviours.

Sharon's determination to believe in herself when no one else did fuels the fire in her belly, becoming a member of a Brisbane based Domestic Violence Charity's, Research and Education Committee and Advocate.

Sharon was invited to co-present the 'Top 10 Strategies to Rebuilding Your Life after Domestic and Family Violence' and Co-Chair the Lived Experience Sessions at the 2019 Stop Domestic Violence Conference as well as Co-author and returning author in two of the Charity's Anthology's – Thriving Survivors Stories from a Lived Experience

Sharon went onto create the Sharon Le Fort – Speaker * Author * Coach, Service.

Sharon has collaborated as a co-author of five anthologies sharing her insights and wisdom in the hope to empower women of all backgrounds to identify, define and gain clarity and purpose of what's next in their lives.

Sharon's **Mission** is to facilitate the healing and guide those who are forgotten survivors of childhood domestic and family abuse and **De-stigmatize** the impact of childhood domestic and family abuse, mental health, and dissociative identity disorder.

Website:	www.sharonlefort.com.au
Email:	sharonlefortsspeakerauthorcoach@gmail.com
Facebook:	@sharonlefortspeakerauthorcoach
Instagram:	@sharonlefortspeakerauthorcoach
LinkedIn:	www.linkedin.com/in/sharonlefort

CHAPTER 9

Steph Gobraiel

The power of family: Re-defining success

To my beautiful daughter Mariam for teaching me to trust myself wholeheartedly and be the woman and mother that I was always meant to be. After all, if it is to be, it is up to me.

And to my husband Tim, for always supporting me, and for your devotion to our family.

I grew up in Sydney, Australia and I am a first-generation Australian. Both my parents came from Lebanon to escape the civil war to make a better life for themselves. Even living in a new country, my parents held tightly to their beliefs and traditions.

Especially the belief of how boys are more competent than girls. This is very common in the Lebanese culture.

That is why I felt I was the black sheep of the family; I always had my own opinion and I didn't agree with many of the traditions and customs of my parents' heritage. It wasn't common for girls to have their own opinion. I always knew who I was going to be and it wasn't going to be what they wanted. For example, my dad would say "You can be independent when you get married" and I'd say "why only then?" and he would reply, "that's my rules and our tradition".

At the age of 14, I started working, partly because my dad wanted me to understand the value of making money, and the other part (for me) was the opportunity to speak to all different people, from all walks of life.

Looking back, starting to work at an early age set me up with great life skills such as customer service, how to manage my money, systems and processes, all of which have been major foundations for my future jobs. It helped me develop an independent mindset.

I lived on my own for ten years and it opened my eyes to a whole new world. My lived experience was made up of travel, representing Australia at an Asia Pacific Summit for work, falling in love with the right and wrong people, and it showed me that family can be created with whom you surround yourself with. It also showed me the corporate world was largely made up of boys' clubs, which is part of why I want to empower women who are in business.

Fast forward a decade to when I met my husband, Tim. I hadn't met anyone before who thought as I did - someone wanting to forge their own path. He wasn't afraid to be with a strong, ambitious, and independent woman like me and wasn't intimidated by it. It took some time for it to sink in but I'd met my match, and it was an amazing feeling. At this point in my life, I thought finally being "settled down" would improve my relationship with my family... it didn't.

After four years of marriage, we had a beautiful baby girl. This was the earth-shattering, pivotal moment of my life. Again, nothing had changed with my family so it was time to cut the cord. My focus was going to be on this beautiful life I created and give her all my energy and time. Nothing can prepare you for this change in direction yet it was empowering. My husband has always been supportive throughout all of this change and encouraged me to follow my instincts and dreams and grow a business that worked around our family life.

Now, all I want to be is a role model for my daughter and I want her to be proud of her mum more than anything in this world. That is why I'm writing this chapter because when you have a child, your perspective on life changes and I want to share the incredible lessons that I learned along the way. Educating and empowering yourself is amazing, but often, simply knowing there is someone else out there that has been through what you're going through, can bring about huge change.

The Challenges

Even though I had a good childhood, parts of it were challenging. Constantly butting heads and being put in my place by my dad was hard.

I always felt lost about my heritage. If I said I'm Australian, people would say "no you're Lebanese" and then when I went overseas, I was called Australian... WHAT THE... Who was I then?

It was a confusing time. I, therefore, went through high school with a lot of uncertainty. I was bullied in school, in year seven for being a 'goody goody'. And it wasn't until I came face to face with my bully that I realised no one was coming to help me but ME.

After I finished school, I decided to leave home and the reaction from my family was like I was the first person to ever leave home. After all, a good Lebanese girl didn't leave home until she was married . I was in a push-pull situation where I was never going to be the person my parents wanted me to be and they couldn't accept who I was, so I had to leave.

The challenges kept coming as an adult. I never thought in a million years I'd leave the corporate world. I was very successful because of my ambition, drive etc. but I knew I had to make the best decision for myself and my daughter to leave so that I could have control over my work-life balance.

Going from being around hundreds of people daily to being at home with a baby felt isolating. Without family support and with Tim being at work from the time the sun came up till it set made it even harder.

I had no idea what to expect or what to do and adding 'mum brain' to it all didn't help. Day turned into night and night turned into day for a while.

The outside noise and decisions.

My daughter only slept either next to me or on my chest, so I was exhausted all the time. People judged me and I received so many unwanted and unhelpful opinions, that I hired a sleep consultant who showed me the 'rock to sleep and then put your baby down' method. After a week of ignoring her cries, my daughter stopped smiling at me when she woke up and it broke my heart. I ended up telling Tim to lie and say, if anyone asks, she sleeps, eats, and does what she should. I regret doing this now, but at the time I didn't know better. I was just desperate to get everyone to stop offering me advice.

It was a pivotal moment for me. There is nothing more special than your baby waking up and smiling at you and an 'expert' had made me doubt my intuition and had taken that away from me so, I learnt to keep quiet and trust myself. Every child is different and there is no right or wrong way of parenting if it comes from a place of love.

My health suffered because I was the primary caretaker with no family support and at that point, I didn't have time to think about what I needed. I kept going and as long as I was upright, that was enough for me.

At the 12-month mark, my maternity leave ended and I had to decide as to whether I was going to go back to the corporate world and work 10/12 hour days or put being a mum first. It wasn't an easy decision. I'd built my career to a high point but I knew my daughter would always come first and I didn't want to regret missing out on the special moments in her life.

I needed to start doing something for myself because I can be the first to admit, I'm not built to be a stay-at-home mum. Initially, I started selling vitamins but I didn't like pushing products on people, it just wasn't me. After further research, I discovered the virtual assistant world. However, that's where I met this monster called mum guilt. A monster that no one talks about enough.

A whole new world.

I decided it was time to put my daughter into daycare when she was sixteen months old.. Because she'd only known me as her carer, it was hell. I would leave with her screaming and would get in the car, shaking, crying, and feeling like someone was stabbing me in both ears with steak knives. I would sit there for ten minutes, and then call the daycare to make sure she was settled before I could leave. The mum guilt was like a wave, and worst of all, I knew I'd experience that wave the next day too.

After calming myself down, I would rush home, excited to turn into 'work Steph' where I could finally use my brain and make money again. I feel guilty saying it, but that version of me felt free.

However, it was really hard because I wouldn't see anyone all day, then be on mum duty again; that was it. There was no time for anything else. Alongside that was the 'normal' entrepreneur fear of not succeeding.

Listening to our bodies and the universe.

I genuinely believe the universe sends you messages and it's our job to pay attention to them. One of these messages came in the form of a flyer in my mailbox. It was for a co-working hub that was opening up close by. I was so excited at the concept of seeing people again so I went for a tour and loved it. I decided that would be my new office.

It meant I could have conversations with other business owners and not feel isolated like I did at home. Even though I was speaking with people online, I still felt very much alone. This simple change made such a difference to my mindset and my productivity.

My daughter was the motivation I needed to make my new lifestyle work. Remembering why I was doing this made me work hard and make decisions based on what we needed as a family. I learnt that when I listened to my gut about my daughter, things worked out. It wasn't easy because there was a lot of background noise which tried to get in the way, but I know there is an unwavering power in being a mum. It's like it gives us superpowers.

Don't get me wrong, listening to logic is important and wise, but if our instincts are telling us to do something it's important to listen, otherwise, you might find yourself learning the hard way that you should have trusted yourself at the beginning.

I also recognised I needed to make time for my health. I made that time during 'work' hours because it's what worked for me and it's my business, so no one but me dictates what I do and when. We need to give ourselves permission to do what works best for us as individuals.

The business wake-up call.

When I was two years into my business, I realised I wasn't attracting the clients I wanted; I was attracting more corporate-style clients. The incredible business community I'd become a part of, told me I needed to trust myself and re-brand. I needed to serve the clients that felt right for me and not just chase the money.

Working out of a co-working hub gave me the confidence I needed. It felt like a community and I'd recommend any entrepreneur to find one too. Their collective knowledge and support have become invaluable to me over the years.

Unfortunately, I was still suffering from health conditions at that time. I'm still working through health issues today due to my neglect for three plus years. This was a huge lesson that I'm still dealing with today.

Putting Self-care and boundaries first.

This year, one of my biggest focuses is self-care because as a mum, it's very easy to put yourself last. I grew up hearing "you put family first" so it was a big mindset shift for me, but they normally do take time to recognise.

The mum's guilt continues to come in waves and that's something I need to accept as it won't change. HOWEVER, someone wise told me the guilt comes from a place of love and I've learnt if I need to cry, I should get it out of my system. It's not something I can control in that moment, and I shouldn't have to, anyway. Having kids, juggling a business, and home life is like having two and a half full-time jobs and admitting it's overwhelming sometimes, that is OK.

Just like when having kids, there is no manual for starting or building a business. Your skills and personality are unique and so that's how your business will be too. It's not easy but with courage, persistence and grit to keep going, you'll succeed where others fail.

I've also learnt that we're a reflection of our business so that's another reason why we should be looking after ourselves, otherwise, we can't give to our kids, our businesses or to anything else.

I now make sure I communicate with Tim when I need help because I now recognise that I'm one person and can't do it all on my own. I tried and it cost me my health. It's not a sign of weakness to ask for help, it's how you grow and excel.

These lessons have become my WHY in business. I know how selfless mums are and I know I can use my expertise as an Online Business Manager to help their business run with more processes and structure, whilst helping them build their visibility so they can have more quality family time. I want to be that positive change for mums in businesses so that they can take school holidays without their laptops and enjoy their evenings without paperwork. Kids grow up so fast and nothing is forever, and we can't risk missing out on a single second with them.

It's also important to remind female entrepreneurs to make time to look after themselves because when you're running on the hamster wheel of your own business, no one tells you to pause or make time for yourself and that's key if you want a successful business and a life of good health and vitality.

Key Learnings.

My key learnings from my last four and a half years being a mum and in business are:

1. Trust what your gut and body tell you because nothing will be closer to the truth.

2. Whatever you feel, it's ok and it's better to let it out – in whatever way works for you – it can be crying, dancing, or going for walks in nature.

3. Be open to the fact that business growth comes from personal growth.

4. Coming out of your comfort zone is always going to be scary but it's the only way to grow.

5. Be kind to yourself because it all starts with you.

6. Whatever you're going through is temporary, it's not forever even though it may feel that way at the time. It's about creating calm from chaos in life and in business.

Trust what your gut and body tell you because nothing will be closer to the truth.

Mums have a built-in radar that should NEVER be ignored. When I was pressured into getting a sleep consultant, everything in me was screaming "no" and when I noticed my baby daughter had stopped smiling at me, it felt like someone had ripped my heart out of my body. However, when I stopped that method, trusted myself, and let her sleep on my chest again, she woke up smiling and I can't put into words how that felt. It was such a sense of overwhelming happiness and joy. This lesson isn't just for babies. Even when your kids grow and go to school, listen to what your body tells you and you can't go wrong.

Whatever emotions you are feeling, it's ok and it's better to let it out – in whatever way works for you – it can be crying, dancing, going for walks in nature – whatever works best for you.

I would go for walks and listen to music that I love to pick up my mood which really helped. I find music to be like medicine and I love to throw in a dance move or two along the way!

Be open to the fact that business growth comes from personal growth.

You can find that growth by finding a coach to help you work through mindset blocks. I listened to a lot of podcasts (such as the Online Business Lift-Off), to get started, which gave me great tips for every area of business.

Coming out of your comfort zone is always going to be scary but it's the only way to grow.

Being an ex-executive assistant, I always ran the show from behind the scenes and the General Managers would be front and centre. However, I now realise that because it's my business, I need to be the one at the front. Showing your personality is how you build the trust factor with people online. I also try to do one thing per quarter which pushes me out of my comfort zone which really works for me. It doesn't have to be something huge, little things work too. For example, in 2022 Q1, I re-branded and put my images on my website. Q2, I started doing videos - this took some time to build the courage to do this! Q3, I applied for two awards. I didn't realise the power of becoming a finalist and what that can do for your business. In Q4, I started delivering Masterclasses. Has it been easy? No. Am I learning and growing from it? Absolutely.

Be kind to yourself because it all starts with you.

As a mum, sometimes our self-care doesn't even make the to-do list, but leaving ourselves off it always affects our families, businesses, and everything else that we do. It's not easy to put yourself first now and again. I've made a conscious decision to focus on my health for 2023 and get it to where it needs to be again. I've started painting because I find it therapeutic, and I schedule self-care into my business diary every week because I find that's the only way, I make the time and stick to it.

Whatever you're going through is temporary, it's not forever even though it may feel that way at the time. It's about creating calm from chaos in life and business.

I believe calm starts with you. Sometimes tough periods can feel like they'll never end, but reminding ourselves "we will get through it, I need to take one day at a time, even this will pass", can help. It's about creating balance and making sure it works for you and your family first, then business second. If it's not working at home, it will eventually take a toll on your business. I genuinely believe everything happens for a reason and we might not know what that reason is, but the universe has many clever ways of changing your direction so you end up on the right path. But only if you listen, trust your gut, and make the changes when you need to.

....Good girls don't make history, bold people make history..... You have to make choices that might be contrary to what you've heard and that's empowerment and it might not come from your parents it has to come from you.

Priyank Chopra

Lots of love

Steph xoxo

Steph Gobraiel

Steph Gobraiel is a highly experienced online business manager and founder of Virtual Associate Services. As a former executive assistant to high-level corporate managers, she has a wealth of experience and business knowledge. Steph has worked with big corporates such as Westpac, CPA Australia and Intel, and holds a Diploma in Business Administration and Management.

As an OBM, Steph helps small business owners create effective habits to run their businesses more efficiently. Her sound advice streamlines business operations, and Steph specialises in helping her clients build impressive online profiles.

Steph is dedicated to supporting women in business. She believes seeking business support is a sign of strength and growth. With practical support and the right mix of empathy, wisdom and accountability, Steph helps coaches, creatives and consultants untangle their business knots and create a sustainable plan for the future.

With a passion for helping owners build their businesses around their families, Steph helps overwhelmed entrepreneurs say goodbye to exhaustion and hello to a successful business (that doesn't take over every moment of their lives).

Steph was a finalist in the Women's Organisation (Creating Change for Women) category of the 2022 Australian Small Business Champion Awards and in the Solopreneur category of the 2022 Roar Awards.

With her depth of experience and expertise, Steph is a trusted adviser in helping her clients achieve their goals and reach their full potential. And as a dynamic and driven individual, she is a valuable virtual team member for the modern small business.

Website: www.virtualassociateservices.com.au
Email: steph@virtualassociateservices.com.au
Facebook: @Virtualassociateservices
Instagram: @steph_gobraiel.obm
LinkedIn: www.linkedin.com/in/stephanie-gobraiel
Guide: mailchi.mp/ed1af2f6dbc2/7-things-to-get-your-business-started

CHAPTER 10

Terri Tonkin

Living on purpose

"Enlightenment does not mean making the most of bad situations. It means knowing that every situation is neither good nor bad." ~ Mokokoma Mokhonoana

How do you live your life? Does your work bring you joy? Do you live from a place of scarcity or from abundance? What do you do, each day, to fill your cup?

These are not easy questions for most people. We generally go to work, to get an income, to provide for our family and to meet our needs, and at times, our wants. Does this sound familiar?

Terri Tonkin

We get told to go to school, to get educated, get a job, work hard, get married, have a family, buy a house, and do all the 'right' things.

I know for me, it was like this for way too many years. As a child, I had a dream. My dream was to write a book. My dream was put aside, for many reasons. I finished school, I got a job (which I thought was going to be my career), got married, had my children, bought a house, supported my husband in his career and career changes, and worked to have a second income to meet our family and financial needs and wants, to have a 'good' life.

I have had some amazing experiences and I have had some great jobs. In some jobs, I was happy, I loved my work, and I was enjoying the experience. I have met some wonderful people through my employment journey, and due to my husband's work, we were able live in a number of locations within Australia, and have travelled overseas.

From an early age, I learnt to read, and became an avid reader as a child. I fell in love with many of the Enid Blyton books, The Secret Seven, The Famous Five and many other books. My love of books has stayed with me to this day. I love reading, and always have a book handy, sometimes I have been known to have two or three on the go, at the same time. Through my books, my language has expanded. I have learnt things I am not even aware of at times. I might be in a conversation, and I can offer information or discuss different topics. I have often said to others, "Please don't ask me how I know that. I just do." One of the many benefits of reading.

Alongside reading, I have developed into a life-long learner. I enjoyed school, I enjoy learning new things, I could even go so far as to say I enjoy studying and learning new concepts. My children think I am weird, and maybe I am, when compared to others. And that is okay. I'll own that one. Throughout my employment journey, I was the first to put my hand up for any training opportunities, personal and professional development. It would light up my soul, like I was in my happy place.

The personal and professional development took me on another trajectory. I studied life coaching and then facilitated workshops to share what I had learnt. By sharing information and knowledge, others would get the benefits. Not everyone was interested in what I had to share, and that's okay too. Everybody learns in different ways.

I have worked in the defence forces, retail, taught children to swim, hardware, truck and tractor spares, banking, youth programs, public service and had my own business. I have learnt many skills and gained heaps of varying experiences. It doesn't appear to follow a natural progression to where I am at now. Each employment has taught me skills, provided wisdom and brought me to a place where I knew there was more to my life, than what I was living.

My hubby and I had worked all our married life, except for me for a few years when the boys were little. Our boys had some great holidays, they got to be involved in sport, and lived with different cultures.

The boys grew up, left home and lived their own lives. And I was happy to be an empty nester. Like I said, others think I am a bit weird. I felt my job as a parent was done. I raised and nurtured them, taught them life skills and they were ready to go out on their own, to live life their way.

When I worked in the public service. the work environment had become toxic and I chose to take a redundancy. I had no idea what I would do, yet I knew I couldn't stay. Weird feeling, as I had loved my job, and with so many changes and programs being cut, I was not happy anymore. I was going downhill quite quickly where I had no motivation to get up and go to work. But I did. And it took over six weeks for the approval to be notified to me. The whole process took a toll on my health, both physically and mentally.

As a result, I didn't want to people at all. I didn't want to go out, I didn't want to socialise, I wanted to stay in bed. It took me nearly twelve months to want to venture outside my home. When I did, I took on some volunteer work, and towards the end of the year, I stepped out and attended a weekend training, for free. More personal/professional development to move me forward.

The weekend training took me back into life coaching. My mind and heart were feeling alive and I was living again.

For eighteen months, I committed to completing the training. I wanted the certificate, not for anyone else, but for me. I was a mature-aged woman, coming out of a toxic environment where I had been made to feel incompetent and incapable, and I wanted to prove to myself I was anything but how I had been made to feel.

I succeeded. I was chuffed. I did this while I became my mum's carer, and everything that entailed.

So, what's next? I had started my coaching business and was facilitating workshops, I had started my own meet-up group, and there was something missing. I spoke to a mentor, who was a book coach, and I told her I wanted to write my book. From a childhood dream, to reality, at age 60. My mentor asked me, "Why now?" My response was, "I've run out of excuses."

AN ENLIGHTENED *Life*

I don't consider myself, or identify, as a religious or spiritual person, yet I had a knowing. I knew I had to write my book, so my grandchildren would have my story, and so my mum could read it while she still could.

You see, Mum had dementia, and it was escalating. She was in care, and she had some okay days, and she had some horrible days. I was on a mission to have this book written and published, for mum to hold it in her hands, and be able to read it. I wanted her to know, I had achieved my dream.

Within three months, the book was written and published, and soon after, printed and delivered.

My dream had come true. I had written my book; I was a published author.

That little book, changed my life.

Who knew how my life would change, so much?

I continued with my coaching, and my meetup group, and being mum's carer. With so much going on at the same time, I started to lose myself. I loved what I was doing, yet it didn't give me the same pleasure and joy it had in the beginning. Something was missing.

The following year, I was invited to contribute to a compilation book, a business book. Me, writing in a business book!!!! I did have a little chuckle to myself. As much as I loved what I did, I didn't like the business side of things. To have a business, you need to do the business side of things, whether you want to, or not. Funny that, can't have one without the other.

Anyway, I contributed my chapter, and drew on my coaching skillset and wrote about perceptions in business. My journey, for all the zigs and zags, had paid off.

Later that year, my mum succumbed to the dementia, and she passed away, with my brother and I by her side. I stepped away from everything. I took time to grieve, to reassess where I wanted to be and what I wanted to do.

Early the next year, hubby was made redundant and a month later, the world imploded with the pandemic. What was I going to do now? I had decided I didn't want to go back into business, yet I didn't know what to do. I had to keep my mind occupied and I didn't want to be swept up in the fear that was building around me.

An opportunity came my way, to contribute a chapter to another compilation, and soon after, another opportunity. Different topics, different audiences. Again, my life journey provided the material, through lived experiences.

The next year, two more writing opportunities came my way. Can you see the pattern happening here? The next phase of my life, was finding me. Writing. I was loving it.

From my dream as a little girl, to write my own book, to becoming a published author in my own right, and contributing to the books compiled by others. I was now living my dream. What a journey I had been on.

Later in the year, I attended some training delivered by a ghostwriter. I had been following his social media for some time, and the training he provided had me hooked. This was how I could continue to write, and be compensated for my work. Within a month of proclaiming my shift of direction, I had signed my first ghostwriting client. I was blessed, with the timing and the client. My new life was taking shape.

By January of the new year, I had completed my first manuscript for my client. I had signed a second client, and had committed to more compilation books. I was asked to help people write their resumes. I was asked to write travel blogs. I was approached to write content for websites, and to rewrite articles of interest. I have done reviews and rewrites for other authors. I was even asked if I would do copywriting. My response was no. I had considered following that path, did some free training and soon realised, copywriting was not my forte. Definitely not my forte. And that is okay. I knew when to walk away, even though it would have been a lucrative option.

This year has been one of the best, most productive years for me. Seven compilation books. Three manuscripts for ghostwriting clients, piece work for clients, plus published in two magazines. I truly believe next year will be even better.

I have committed to three more compilation books already. I have said no, to four others. As I write for others, their work is my priority. This is not to say I will only do client work. I will write for myself, and for others. Work/life balance, or as I prefer, work/life harmony. I can have both, I can do both.

As I said earlier, I do not refer to myself as religious or spiritual. I do follow my heart, and have a knowing of what is best for me, in the moment.

I tend to live in the moment, I am not a great planner. I set intentions, yet not specific goals. I know that goes against the grain of many thought leaders and coaches. It is what works for me. If it doesn't feel right for me, if it doesn't fit into my life, why put myself into situations where it is not going to bring joy and happiness.

I choose to be happy. I choose to have joy in my life. I choose to do what makes me feel good about the work I do, and the benefits it brings to my clients and to myself. Life is full of choices, and we all get to make those choices. If you decide not to make a choice, you have made a choice. Funny that.

I saw this quote recently, and totally got it.

"I am at a place in my life where peace is a priority. I make deliberate life choices to protect my mental, emotional and spiritual state." ~ Unknown.

I am at a point in my life, where I am blessed with the life journey I have been on, including the good, the bad and the ugly. My life hasn't been perfect; I don't think anyone can claim that. My life has been full of love, adventure, good times, not so good times, sadness, happiness, achievement, learnings and so much more. When it is all wrapped up into a package, you get me.

Before I wrote this chapter, I went looking for definitions of 'enlightened'. This is what I found:

Enlighten – to give information or understanding; to free from superstition; bring information to light; dispelling ignorance

Enlightened – rational and having beneficial effects: tolerant and unprejudiced.

I hope and trust, through my writing, I provide information and understanding, create conversation and encourage free thinking. In the past, I know I have been intolerant and prejudiced, and these things I have worked on over many years. I also know, there are times when this still happens. Some things trigger me, and get under my skin. This tells me I have more to learn, and there are alternative ways to deal with matters as they arise.

AN ENLIGHTENED *Life*

I am a mature-aged woman, with lived experiences, who has been on a journey of discovery, of self and others, to reach the point in my life, where I am grateful and happy and blessed.

I am successful in my own right, although it may not be in the same realm you believe to be success, as that in itself, is a whole other dimension. Success is different for each and every person.

I live my life on my terms. I don't seek or need approval from others. I am fortunate to be living my life, on purpose, through my writing for myself and others. It took many years to achieve my dream. I am grateful for the life journey I have travelled, the people I have met, and the experiences I have had.

I believe, if you can work at what you love, you will always have joy and happiness in your life. If you can find what you are passionate about, whatever it is that lights you up, follow that light.

You may be fortunate to find many things you enjoy on your life journey. Experience as many as you can. Bring the joy into your life, as it will spread to others.

I know and understand I am not everyone's cup of tea. I don't have to be.

"Life is a sum of all your choices." ~ Albert Camus

Terri Tonkin

Connect Within

Have you ever wanted to write your book, and share your story?

Terri Tonkin knows how this feels, because as a child, she had always wanted to write her own book. She achieved this dream at the young age of 60.

Terri is a multiple International Best Selling Author, Ghostwriter and life coach. She has written her own book, contributed to 14 compilation books and is now writing manuscripts for others.

Terri has been featured in The Corporate Escapists and Disruptive Publishing magazines and has been interviewed on Voices on Fire; Empowered to Shine; Fast Forward Your Entrepreneur Journey and The Corporate Escapists podcasts.

She is the face of Connect Within, and her clients are heard, validated, acknowledged, encouraged and supported to find the solutions they are searching for.

Terri aspires to inspire the people she meets to reach their potential, as inspiration leads to motivation, and motivation leads to action, providing results.

Her life has been a journey of ups and downs, trials and tribulations, both personally and professionally. She is a life-long learner, seeks out new opportunities, is an avid reader and loves to travel.

Facebook: www.facebook.com/connectwithinmindsetlifecoach/
Email: terri@connectwithin.com.au
LinkedIn: www.linkedin.com/in/terri-tonkin/
Website: www.connectwithin.com.au

Tracey Horton

International award winning author of The Unhappy Smile, Life mentor, mentoring women all over the world - Gold Coast, Australia.

CHAPTER 11

Tracey Horton

Your purpose is always in a season

They say when we get to the end of our days, we will recall only the best of our memories and wish for more of them.

I am a big believer in living a life that's rich and full, so that when it's my time to sit in the chair with all my memories, I have more to recant than I have days left to live.

One such memory will be of The Bellagio in Las Vegas.

I found myself there a few years back to sign with the Las Vegas Speakers Bureau, travelling with my son in law we decided we had to do a Facebook live at midnight in front of the musical fountain and honestly the feeling you experience in my opinion is worth it being added to your "must do" bucket list.

But tonight the memory I will hold for the rest of my life happened inside at the bar.

The Bellagio is opulence personified, from the moment you enter greeted by staff in suits, to walking through their current display, which was Christmas for us as we were there early December, to being led to a luxurious velvet seat at the bar, all five of your senses are feasting.

Dylan and I were cold from being outside, so we settled at the bar for a drink., As I ordered, the young man serving us asked about the book I was holding. I explained my story and how I wrote a book to help others overcome whatever they have gone through, I then signed it and gave it to him as my gift. The next moments will forever bring tears to my eyes, he looked into my eyes and said "thank you, I will give it to my mum, she needs to read this, thank you for coming in, we don't get amazing people like you at our bar."

I instantly choked up, beginning the Internal dialogue "don't cry Tracey, don't make this weird."

What no one else at that bar except my Son-in-law knew was that I grew up abused, beaten and impoverished. he thought that one day I would be in a place like The Bellagio was unthinkable, let alone the experience of loving kindness I was just having.

At that moment I knew something deeper and stronger than ever before – I was created for a deep, divine purpose, which, while it isn't always clear for me, the Universe, God, the angels are always with me, to see my purpose work out in this lifetime.

Great news, your life is fully backed and designed with purpose for great success.

AN ENLIGHTENED *Life*

Enlightened lives understand that life is fluid, that we are always in season, that every season we live through is designed to be knitted together to ensure our success.

3 things are true of your life right now:

1. You are alive

2. You're reading this book

3. There is a purpose in you that history will record.

Right now stop and think of all the people that we remember throughout history, not one of them didn't leave it all on the field, they all came to play, they addressed issues, righted wrongs, changed cultural mindsets and left us all better off for it.

Some of you know that you know that you have a huge purpose in this lifetime to effect, love and change the planet before you leave. But everyone has a story and it is unique to you, there is never a person before you or after you in history that will have your unique life, and that uniqueness is where your purpose is found

There is a divine purpose in knowing that for many of us, our purpose also includes raising children that will go on to live out their fullest purpose.

The best story to remind us of this is certainly the story of Einstein's mother, let me paraphrase it for you, who was presented with a note from the teacher at school by her son one afternoon and after reading it, when asked by her eager son what it said she replied " the teacher sees that you have a great gift of knowledge and she feels she has taught you everything she can, so starting tomorrow you will stay home and I will school you". The point of the story is that when his mum passed, Einstein found the original letter and it read "I regret to inform you that your son is a constant disruption in my class and displays signs of not being able to learn, I therefore need him removed from school for the sake of the other children."

I love this story because the only child we have ever heard of from that class is Einstein.

It doesn't matter what traditional learning says, every child has a purpose, some of them to change the world as we know it.

I believe that in all our purposes we are called to support each other. No one raises to all they can be without a support team, the biggest world changers all had support teams.

I have a friend in my life called Julie and I can honestly say hand on heart, my life purpose flourishes because she so lovingly has my back. When I am tired she organises a spa day, when I get invited to speak overseas, she books the flights, hotels, etc and always travels with me because I hate travelling alone. When I take the stage she is in the front row, cheering me on , ever reminding me, everybody is a part of something purposeful.

Every minute of our lives we are in season. With everyday we live, something about our future is being written, many times by our past.

Discerning and living present in the current chapter of your life is the biggest key to navigating life successfully. You only need to be willing, willing makes you open, willing makes you step out, willing makes you bold and courageous.

We live on a planet that is governed by the law of seasons. Everything in nature has a process of seasons, and so do we. It's important for us to understand we are tri-part beings, body, soul and spirit and as such we are governed by the same laws of the universe, just as all of creation.

AN ENLIGHTENED *Life*

There is a season for everything, understanding where you are, will help you to define your purpose.

There are signs that we all know exist yet avoiding them seems to be something we all do.

If you find yourself in a season of preparation, it's the time to notice change, see things moving forward to give us growth and change. This season is about shedding, the more we can feel into it, the easier it will bring us into the next season of winter. The preparation in this season will determine how long and hard winter will be. When we find ourselves in this season, the requirement is surrender, letting go of what we are holding and allowing the lesson to appear.

Let's call this season Autumn, where we are energetically feeling things are changing. We notice things are brought to our attention that need dealing with.

There is a definite sense of preparation in your mind which can be making you uncomfortable in situations and with people you were once comfortable with.

Your soul and spirit are uneasy when you are alone, not sure why, you want to start to withdraw, to think.

This season will automatically slide you into the next season of Winter which is our season of pain, of loss, and of pruning. This is when we let go no matter what, because it's the time to say goodbye to everything not serving us anymore. This season is lonely, this is all about you and only you can do the work required for the new growth. Others can encourage you but it's you that decides what stays and bears new buds in the next season of spring from here. Much like the grapes being crushed to make wine, we can feel very broken and hurt in this season. When we find ourselves here the requirement is truth that leads to vulnerability. Vulnerability is a superpower but only when we let it lead us to the truth we must learn. This winter season, remember that while this is the hardest of the seasons you will go through, it's the most important season, without this season of pruning, there is no healthy growth.

This is the time to let go of what isn't working, finding ways to deal with things, and while there is definitely a sense of loss, a desire to hibernate, avoid the big issues coming up and becoming acutely aware of needing to survive, the gift of this season is teaching us the strength of being lonely, hesitant, finding the courage unsure of outcome but make the call anyway. Every inch of courage you own, was birthed in this season.

This season is about coming to terms that it is done, it has died, it is the end of your part of being in this story. Every person will experience loss, we all have a chapter in our books called 'The things we didn't get back'." There is no miracle coming, it's out of your hands and you are left with just a heart of grief and sadness. This is not what you wanted, not how you saw it and you aren't ready for it.

The key to this stage is knowing you must grieve and allow that however it shows up.

The key to this stage is allowing the truth of it being over, to settle.

The key to this stage is once hope is gone, we must find it again. We must start to write the next chapter different than we expected, but our book isn't done.

Great news, this season ends and is followed by what we call Spring, this is the season where it is the time we get stretched, we grow.

AN ENLIGHTENED *Life*

Now growth is vital but not always pleasant because we always feel pain when we are stretched for our new purpose.

While in this stage, we are exactly like teenagers with growing pains, necessary but painful. Emotional pain is always hard as it requires that we process it for ourselves, life is 10% what happens to you and 90% how you deal with it. This stage requires a fresh commitment to back yourself, to be your greatest advocate. To realise that you must have your own back.

Now is when you need to set new intentions, choose the new path, decide the positive from what you have been through. This is the start of something great, you and others can see growth in and around you.

Which leads perfectly Into what we can call Summer.

This is the season of relaxed rewards, it's when we enjoy all that came from the season of change and growth. This season is one to be felt with love and joy, never to be underplayed or ignored because others around us aren't in their summer. When we get to this season we need to rest, relax, enjoy, celebrate, we have changed, conquered, endured, healed or transformed and being positive in celebrating that puts a strong subconscious story into our minds that will see us more able to do the full process next time.

It is now that you will start seeing the rewards of working through the other stages, experiencing success. Now is the time to be open to new possibilities and relationships.

Once we understand these seasons, able to see and know where you are, you can allow it to do whatever it needs to do to create the path of purpose in your life.

We go through these chapters/seasons all our lives, sometimes all four within a month. Sometimes each of them for a year or more.

They can be in relation to anything in life, relationships, business, unfulfilled desires, broken dreams.

It's not if, but when they show up, so the most important thing is to prepare yourself because once we are real in our knowledge, we are empowered with our choices.

Purpose will take everything you have, at the same time making the life you live everything it's meant to be.

At times when you can see that freedom of purpose isn't possible, right now where you are, then it's time to make strong changes, otherwise this is always going to be the way it is. If you are in a relationship that's hard, calling you to compromise who you are, aware you will always lose, this is when YOU need to just let go, it doesn't mean you don't still care, you aren't still hurting, you still wish it was different, but it can't be ever what you want.

This is hard as our hearts stay very connected even after our heads make the decision.

The key at this stage is recognising patterns, and they will be there if you look deep enough.

The process is letting go because you alone cannot change it, so it needs to leave your life so something better can come.

This wasn't meant to be, it was a chapter not the whole story.

But when we can see that there is change required, there is a cost to be paid, but it is worth the cost, wisdom calls us to see

AN ENLIGHTENED *Life*

the things that can be changed, sorted, fixed, mended, even to the point of exhaustion, then hope arrives making you want to give it a go again.

This is when you will need to change, grow, expand or upskill to move and heal the situation, this should be done and is always well worth it.

I can physically hear you begging me to tell you how to tell the difference, yet you already know the answer.

We always know, we just don't listen to our deep inner voice as much as we should. Intuitively you know if it should end, you should fight for it.

If you weren't frustrated then you wouldn't be living your purpose. There is never a better time, there is only time. There is never a set way, only your unique path, that absolutely leads to extraordinary, excellent, massive success.

Enlightened people understand the most misunderstood, underappreciated universal truth, **they cannot possibly fail**.

Let me leave you with this quote from Mark Twain.

"If everybody was satisfied with himself there would be no heroes." —Mark Twain

You have got this magnificent unique human and you will leave your mark.

Love Tracey

Tracey Horton

Tracey Horton is an inspiration to all that meet her.

Born into a home of poverty, domestic violence and sexual abuse, her story reads like a horror story, abused by 12 men and left to raise herself while her mum had a breakdown all before 14 years of age.

Told at 18 that she was so mentally broken that she couldn't contribute to society and would probably be dead by 30.

She began a definitive journey of self-discovery and healing and today is an international speaker ,mentor and educator who teaches emotional strength, resilience and self-leadership through courses and events worldwide.

Tracey is a wealth of knowledge and wisdom, she is easy to listen to with a combination of a profound life knowledge and a down to earth attitude.

She is an International award winning author of The Unhappy Smile.

She is a life mentor, mentoring women all over the world.

She lives on the Gold Coast with her husband Paul, she has 4 grown daughters who are all married and 9 grandchildren .

Her life mantra is "Never write your story in someone else's handwriting."

Facebook: @traceyhorton8
Instagram: @traceyhorton8
LinkedIn: @traceyhorton-CEO
Website: www.traceyhorton.com

www.ingramcontent.com/pod-product-compliance
Lightning Source LLC
Chambersburg PA
CBHW041143110526
44590CB00027B/4111